A–Z

OF

PLYMOUTH

PLACES - PEOPLE - HISTORY

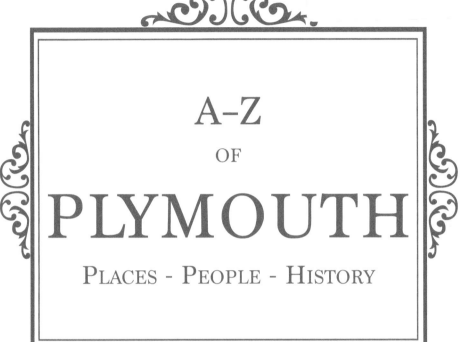

Derek Tait

AMBERLEY

First published 2020

Amberley Publishing
The Hill, Stroud, Gloucestershire, GL5 4EP
www.amberley-books.com

Copyright © Derek Tait, 2020

The right of Derek Tait to be identified as
the Author of this work has been asserted in
accordance with the Copyrights, Designs and
Patents Act 1988.

ISBN 978 1 4456 9658 4 (print)
ISBN 978 1 4456 9659 1 (ebook)

British Library Cataloguing in Publication Data.
A catalogue record for this book is available
from the British Library.

Typesetting by Aura Technology and Software
Services, India. Printed in Great Britain.

Contents

Introduction

Plymouth is steeped in history, from the prehistoric remains discovered at Cattedown to the Bronze Age trading settlement at Mount Batten. Not forgetting the Roman burial grounds at Stonehouse, the Pilgrim Fathers' departure from the Mayflower Steps, the hard-fought battles of the Civil War and the Blitz during the Second World War.

Many historic buildings can be found within the city including Smeaton's Tower, the Citadel, the Merchant's House, the Elizabethan House and St Andrew's Church, all with interesting tales about Plymouth's fascinating past.

Many streets have historic connections with famous people, including Durnford Street's link with Sir Arthur Conan Doyle, Union Street's connection to Houdini and Laurel and Hardy, Outland Road's link to Robert Falcon Scott, and Tor Lane's affinity to Alexander Graham Bell.

With strong associations with Nancy Astor, Sir Francis Drake, William Bligh, Lawrence of Arabia, Admiral Hardy and Charles Darwin as well as tales of slavers, pirates, suffragettes, mutineers and executions, the city is rich in stories of discoveries, triumphs and disasters, all adding to its compelling history.

The River Tamar from Saltash Passage.

A

Argyle

Plymouth Argyle was founded by two friends, F. Howard Grose and Mr W. Pettybridge, in 1886. Centre back Grose became the club's first captain, but the team had no ground so played their first matches during the 1886/7 season at grounds belonging to their opponents, eventually making their home at a field at Mount Gould.

Plymouth Argyle's ground at Home Park.

The team's first match was played on 16 October 1886, with Argyle losing 2-0 against the Cornish team, Caxton. However, their first win came later in the same week when they beat Plymouth College 2-1.

During the 1889/90 season Argyle found a new home at Marsh Mills before moving to their current ground at Home Park in 1901, which had previously belonged to Devonport Albion Rugby Club.

In 1903, Plymouth Argyle became a professional football club with a limited liability company being formed under the watchful eye of local businessman Clarence Spooner. At the end of the year the team was accepted into the Southern League, with Frank Brettell becoming their first manager as a professional outfit. In their first professional game they beat West Ham 1-0, later beating Northampton Town 2-0 when they played their first home game on 5 September 1903, drawing a crowd of 4,438.

During the 1912/13 season Argyle became Southern League champions and later, in 1920, joined the Football League Division Three (South) under manager Bob Jack, finishing eleventh in their first season, with crowd numbers rising to 12,765. The team won promotion to Football League Division Two during the 1929/30 season, topping Division Three (South), with spectator numbers often reaching 20,000. Matches were put on hold during the Second World War, with the ground being severely damaged by enemy bombing.

The team found themselves back in Division Three during the 1949/50 season, but returned to Division Two after winning the Division Three (South) title in 1951/52.

Today Argyle remains as popular as it has ever been. It has seen many key events during its lifetime, including beating Pele and his Santos team 3-2 in March 1973 and reaching the semi-final of the FA cup in 1984 before being beaten by Watford 1-0.

Well-loved players over the years have included Moses Russell (1914–30), Paul Mariner (1973–76), Leigh Cooper (1979–90), Gordon Nisbet (1981–87), Tommy Tynan (1983–90), Paul Wotton (1995–2008) and David Friio (2000–05).

Armada

During July 1588, the Spanish Armada set sail from Spain with the aim of restoring Catholic rule within England by overthrowing Elizabeth I, a staunch Protestant. Sir Francis Drake reputedly played bowls on Plymouth Hoe when the Armada was first spotted approaching on 19 July 1588, famously stating that there was still plenty of time to finish the game before seeing off the Spaniards.

At the time, as vice admiral, Drake had the English fleet under his command (answering to Lord Howard of Effingham). As darkness closed, the English fleet pursued the Armada up the English Channel, capturing the Spanish galleon *Rosario* together with Admiral Pedro de Valdés and his crew. The ship contained substantial funds, which were to be used to pay the Spanish army.

The statue of Sir Francis Drake on Plymouth Hoe.

During the night of 29 July, Drake, together with John Howard, coordinated fire ships, which resulted in most of the captains of the Spanish vessels breaking formation, sailing out of Calais into open sea. The following day, Drake was present at the Battle of Gravelines where the Spanish fleet were further damaged before they withdrew north, returning home to Spain with a third of their ships lost.

Astor, Nancy

Nancy Witcher Langhorne was born in Virginia in 1879 and moved to England at the age of twenty-six where she married Waldorf Astor. She entered politics soon after and won her husband's former seat in Plymouth in 1919, becoming the first female MP to sit in the House of Commons. During the Second World War, Nancy Astor was Lady Mayoress of Plymouth, living at No. 3 Elliot Terrace.

Lady Mayoress of Plymouth, Nancy Astor dancing with a sailor on Plymouth Hoe. (Courtesy of the *Western Morning News*)

Al fresco dancing on Plymouth Hoe began during the first week of May in 1941 and was a success from the beginning. The idea was first suggested by the Lord Mayor, Lord Astor. Lady Nancy Astor regularly took part in the gatherings and among her dancing partners was the Duke of Kent. During the war years, the dancing raised people's spirits and brought everyone together.

Noel Coward, who was a friend of the Astors, said at the time, 'After all that devastation, on a Summer evening, people were dancing on the Hoe. It made me cry – the bravery, the gallantry, the Englishness of it!' The dances continued for many years and a huge dance was held on the Hoe at the end of the war to celebrate VE Day.

Lady Astor was well known for her direct way of talking. She once said to Winston Churchill, 'If I was your wife I would give you poison!' to which Churchill replied, 'If I was your husband, I'd drink it!' Lady Astor died in 1964.

Athenaeum Street

Athenaeum Street runs from Citadel Road towards the Crescent and was originally designed by John Foulston, who was also responsible for the original Athenaeum building, which was built during 1818 and featured a Greek Doric-style façade. Known originally as the Plymouth Institution, visitors included the architect George Wightwick and Dr Cookworthy. The museum contained many unusual exhibits including 'four tattoed Maori heads of great rarity' and the Barbican Ducking Chair, which had last been used to punish Nancy Clark, an elderly fisherwoman, for assault and use of bad language. The building was destroyed during the Blitz in 1941 before a new Athenaeum was built in 1961.

Nearby Athenaeum Place originally allowed access to the busy stableyard at the Royal Hotel, which contained twenty-three stalls, fourteen loose boxes, two large harness rooms and three large motor or coach houses for twenty carriages and waggonettes. The hotel's courtesy coach picked up passengers and their luggage from the nearby railway station. The proprietor of the hotel also provided coaches for weddings, excursions and funerals.

Looking up Athenaeum Street towards Plymouth Hoe.

Barbican

The narrow lanes of the Barbican were once the home to seafarers such as Francis Drake, Walter Raleigh, John Hawkins and Captain James Cook. Walk the back streets and you're walking through areas where Britain's heroes once trod.

For hundreds of years, Barbican families lived close to their place of work and there was much congestion on the harbour due to handcarts, crates and piles of fish until the fish market was eventually built in 1892. There were many public houses in the area at one time, some still surviving, including The Admiral McBride, The Faithful Irishman, The Brunswick, The North Country Pink, The East and West Country House, The Welshman's Arms, The Crown and Anchor and The Dolphin.

Above left: Old and new buildings on the Barbican.

Above right: Southside Street on the Barbican.

A memorial recording the leaving place of the Pilgrim Fathers for America in 1620 can be found on the quayside; thousands of people visit the spot every year. The Mayflower Steps were only built in 1934 and the actual leaving spot is some distance further back as much of the harbour was reclaimed and built many years later.

Bedford Street

The original Bedford Street ran from George Street to Old Town Street and Spooner's Corner and was one of the main shopping streets in the city before it was destroyed by enemy bombing during the Second World War. Popular shops situated there included Pophams, whose toy room in 1882 stocked 2,000 dolls, as well as Yeo's who were renowned for their blankets, and Goodbody's, which had men from the Royal Marines' band playing in their restaurant during the afternoon. Other well-loved stores included E. Dingle & Co. Ltd, who were based at No. 32 Bedford Street and Spooner & Co. At the time Dingle's boasted eighty departments and employed over 500 people. They had plans to construct a store similar to Harrods and Selfridges in London before the area was blitzed.

Bedford Street before the heavy bombing of the Second World War.

Bell, Alexander Graham

One of the first telephone installations in the UK was in Plymouth at Tor Grove in Weston Peverel, now known as Pennycross.

Alexander Graham Bell was visiting the town in 1877 to lecture about the invention of the telephone when he stayed at the residence of Robert Bayly. Bayly was elected to the first Devon City Council and was also a Justice of the Peace. His father founded the Marine Biological Association.

While staying with Bayly, Bell installed a telephone line, which connected the house and the gardener's cottage. It remained in use for many years before the apparatus was dismantled and presented to Plymouth Museum.

Alexander Graham Bell was born in 1847 in Edinburgh. Both his mother and wife were deaf, which encouraged him to experiment with hearing devices, eventually leading to his invention of the telephone. Although he is best known for this, he felt that the telephone intruded on his more important scientific research and refused to have one in his study. Throughout his life he referred to himself as a teacher to the deaf rather than the inventor of the telephone.

Bell's preferred salutation when answering the newly invented telephone was 'ahoy-hoy', which derived from the nautical term 'ahoy!' It never caught on, however. Today the phrase is often used by Montgomery Burns in the cartoon *The Simpsons*.

Bell is also credited with the invention of the metal detector in 1881. Bell later said, 'Great discoveries and improvements invariably involve the cooperation of many minds. I may be given credit for having blazed the trail but when I look at the subsequent developments, I feel the credit is due to others rather than to myself.'

In 1888 he became one of the founding members of the National Geographic Society.

Alexander Graham Bell, inventor of the telephone.

Blitz

During the Second World War, the heaviest attacks on the city came in 1941. In the two intensive attacks on 20 and 21 March, 336 people lost their lives. Five further attacks in April brought the toll to 590.

Much of the city centre was obliterated and although many buildings remained among the debris, most were damaged beyond repair. Many of the most popular streets – including Bedford Street, Union Street, Old Town Street, Frankfort Street, Cornwall Street and George Street – were either totally destroyed or severely damaged. Major buildings such as the Guildhall, the Municipal Buildings, St Andrew's Church, Charles Church and the General Post Office were obliterated. Many schools were also hit. These included Plymouth High School for Girls, the Hoe Grammar School and the infant school at Summerland Place. Many churches were destroyed also, including St James the Less, King Street Methodist, St Peter's, George Street Baptist and many others. The bombing was indiscriminate and destroyed anything that got in its way.

Outside the city the bombing was just as devastating, and areas affected included Devonport, Stonehouse, St Budeaux, Swilly and Saltash Passage. Devonport lost many buildings including the post office, the Alhambra Theatre, the Synagogue, the Hippodrome and the Salvation Army headquarters.

Residential houses that were either destroyed or beyond repair amounted to 3,754. Others that were seriously damaged but able to be repaired amounted to 18,398. Houses that were slightly damaged amounted to an additional 49,950.

Many children were packed off to live with relatives, friends or obliging families in safe areas in the countryside. Thousands left on special trains and many saw it as an adventure, while others were upset to leave their parents behind. Lady Astor said at the time, 'What helped the evacuation was that everyone seemed to have a cousin in the country.'

News of the devastation of Plymouth soon reached the rest of the world and gifts arrived from all over the world, particularly from the United States who sent ambulances as well as soft toys, food packages and surgical dressings. The Royal Sailors' Rest received crates of supplies so large that they were unable to get them into the building.

At the end of the war there was a total of 4,448 casualties due to the raids and heavy bombing of the city.

A Plymouth street after the Blitz.

Camera Obscura

In the 1800s a camera obscura stood upon the Hoe, just above where the Belvedere stands today. The small hexagonal building had a camera on top that projected a full-colour picture of the surrounding area, capturing all of its movement, onto a white surface in the darkened room below. The screen was said to be a white tablecloth. The image was reversed so had to be corrected by another lens further down.

The Camera Obscura first appeared on the Hoe in the summer of 1827 and was created by machinist William Sampson. It reopened in the same position on 21 May 1828 and tickets could be bought from a Mr Mark on site while season tickets could be bought direct from Mr Sampson at his address at No. 1 Westwell Street. The obscura was open from 9 a.m. until 7 p.m. whenever the weather was fine.

The Camera Obscura on Plymouth Hoe.

During the violent gales of 12 and 13 November 1840 the obscura was destroyed – apparently for the third time. On 17 November, Mr Sampson appealed to the public for funds so that the contraption could be rebuilt, and on 8 July 1841 it reopened for viewing between 9 a.m. and 6 p.m.

When Mr Sampson died his daughter Elizabeth took over the business, and was entirely dependant on people paying to visit the obscura. She also made money from placing advertising boards around the outside of the small building. The council wanted to persuade Miss Sampson to give up ownership of the obscura and offered her an 8s per week pension for life. The camera obscura was demolished in 1889 while improvements were made to the Hoe. Miss Sampson died the following year, aged seventy-three.

Cattedown Caves

In the autumn of 1886, a limestone cave system was discovered by workers at Cattedown. The following year, the area was explored by local historian R. N. Worth together with landowner Robert Burnard of Cattedown Wharves. The bones of fifteen early humans were found together with the remains of woolly rhinoceros,

The fuel depot at Cattedown where the remains of early man were discovered.

woolly mammoth, deer and lion, all dating from the Ice Age. The remains were approximately 140,000 years old and are the oldest remains of humans discovered in the British Isles. Prehistoric remains have also been found in Ernesettle Woods at Mutley and Keyham as well as at Stonehouse.

The Cattedown items were stored at the Athenaeum, but were destroyed when an incendiary bomb hit the building in 1941. The remaining fragments were sent to the Plymouth Museum and Art Gallery.

Because of the fuel depot, the caverns at Cattedown are, at the moment, off limits to the general public.

Charles Church

Charles I gave his permission for a new church to be built in Plymouth in 1641. When it was completed in 1658 it was known then as The Church of Plymouth, and later just Charles Church. Its tower wasn't completed until 1708, with the spire being made of wood and covered with lead until 1766. Charles Church was situated in Vennel Street until the area was obliterated by heavy bombing in 1941. The council's reconstruction committee decided to demolish the church on 15 June 1953 but it was saved, and on 1 November 1958 Revd J. Allen James dedicated it as a memorial to the 1,200 civilians who lost their lives in the war. Soon after, Alderman G. Wingett, the Lord Mayor, unveiled a commemorative plaque on the north wall.

The remains of Charles Church with the Drake Circus Shopping Centre behind.

Citadel

Work began on the Citadel in 1665 after Charles II recognised Plymouth's important position as a channel port. It was designed by Sir Bernard de Gomme and incorporated an old fort that had been built in the time of Sir Francis Drake. Parts of the earlier Tudor fort were incorporated into the new building, the foundation stone of which was laid by John Granville, 1st Earl of Bath, on 18 July 1666. This stone, inscribed 'Jo Earle of Bathe 1666', is still clearly visible in the wall facing the Hoe.

When complete, the cannons not only faced towards the sea but also towards the town. This was thought to have been to keep the population in order as they had supported the Parliamentarians during the Civil War in the reign of Charles' father, Charles I.

The Citadel is built of locally sourced limestone and the English baroque gateway, which was designed by Sir Thomas Fitz, is made of Portland stone. The gateway originally had a drawbridge over a dry moat, but this was removed during the 1880s.

Right: The entrance to the Royal Citadel.

Below: The walls of the Royal Citadel facing towards Plymouth Sound.

Darwin, Charles

At Devil's Point there is a plaque commemorating HMS *Beagle* setting sail from Barn Pool, at Mount Edgcumbe, which was carrying Charles Darwin. Darwin's journey is mentioned in the *Quarterly Review* of 1840: 'On the 27 November, 1831, the well-manned, well-appointed and well-provided Beagle sailed from Barn Pool, and having circumnavigated the globe, and accomplished all the objects the expedition had in view, as far was practical, she anchored at Falmouth on the 2 October, 1836, after an absence of four years and nine months.'

Darwin had lived in Plymouth for two months before his famous voyage around the world in HMS *Beagle*. The ship was captained by Robert Fitzroy. Darwin, who was then just twenty-two years old, joined the crew as a naturalist. He had a wealthy family who paid the £30 fare needed to travel on the *Beagle*.

Below left: A portrait of Charles Darwin.

Below right: A plaque commemorating Charles Darwin located at Devil's Point.

When he returned to England he married Emma Wedgwood, daughter of the potter Josiah Wedgwood. He carried on his research and in 1859 his book *The Origin of the Species by Natural Selection* was published.

Darwin died in 1882 at his home in Orpington, Kent. He is buried at Westminster Abbey.

Derry's Clock

Before the Second World War, Derry's Clock stood at the junction of George Street, Union Street, Lockyer Street and George Place and was regarded as the centre of the city, with all trams and buses terminating nearby.

The clock was a common meeting place for young sweethearts and was known as the four-faced deceiver because the clocks on all four sides appeared to show different times. The nearby public house was once the city's main Lloyds Bank.

Derry's Clock was presented to the town by William Derry in 1862 and was worth £220, which was half the cost it took to construct the tower to house it. Plymouth didn't have the powers to build a clock, which could only be given by Parliament, so Derry's Clock was officially classed as a fountain, although it was never actually connected to a water supply.

Derry's Clock with the Theatre Royal in the background.

Devil's Point

Devil's Point was originally called Cremhill (Crimble) Point and was so named because of the ancient ferry that carried passengers between there and Cremell (later Cremyll), across the Hamoaze. Originally, the ferry landed at Barn Pool, but in 1730 it was moved to its present landing place at Cremyll because of the upset it caused to the Edgcumbes. The landing place at Cremhill Point was later moved to Mutton Cove in 1750 and sometime after moved to its present location at Admiral's Hard. A Huguenot refugee called Duval took up residence at Devil's Point and some say that this is why the name was changed from Cremhill Point. The name Cremhill Point appears on maps until 1846.

There are three Tudor fortifications to be found in the area of Devil's Point. All date from the time of Henry VIII. They were put in place to defend the mouth of the river. One can be found across the water at Barn Pool, and at one time regular crossings were made there from Western Kings. The two fortifications on the Plymouth side are to be found at Firestone Bay and further around at Eastern Kings, close to the entrance at Millbay. The fortification at Firestone Bay, built in the 1500s, was converted into a restaurant in 1983. Its previous uses had been as a police house, a coastguard station, a store for the Ministry of Defence and a public convenience.

The Chapel of St Lawrence once stood at Devil's Point, but it was removed in the eighteenth century to make way for the Victualling Yard that would later be built there.

Devil's Point looking towards Plymouth Sound.

The view from Devil's Point towards Plymouth Hoe.

The folly at Mount Edgcumbe contains parts of St Lawrence together with parts of the nearby St George Chapel.

Devil's Point still has the remains of defensive posts, pillboxes and anti-aircraft gun emplacements from the Second World War.

Doyle, Arthur Conan

Sir Arthur Conan Doyle assisted at a medical practice at Durnford Street and Sherlock Holmes was said to have been based on his colleague, Dr Budd. Doyle achieved the titles of Bachelor of Medicine and Master of Surgery in 1881 and had studied with George Turnavine Budd at Edinburgh. When Budd opened a practice in Durnford Street in 1882, he asked Doyle to join him. The partnership didn't last long. Although Budd and Doyle were friends, Doyle found his partner overprescribed drugs for his patients, for which he charged them, and was unorthodox in the extreme. He wrote and told his mother, Mary, about Budd's ways. She had never been an admirer of his. After two months the partnership was dissolved because Budd said that it was short of both finances and patients. Doyle discovered later that Budd had found one of his letters to his mother and the real reason for the breakup of the partnership was that he had been upset by what he had read.

Doyle left Plymouth and set up a practice in Southsea with just £10 to his name. At first it wasn't very successful and while he was waiting for patients he wrote his first story featuring Sherlock Holmes, *A Study in Scarlet*.

Doyle died on the 7 July 1930, aged seventy-one. Today, passages from his works featuring Sherlock Holmes can be found on brass plaques set into the pavement at Durnford Street.

Above left: Sir Arthur Conan Doyle, author of the Sherlock Holmes novels. (Courtesy of the Library of Congress)

Above right: A quotation relating to Sir Arthur Conan Doyle set into the pavement at Durnford Street.

Durnford Street

In 1773, the Edgcumbes leased out the land that was later to become Durnford Street and Emma Place. Durnford Street was named after Joan Durnford, the fifteenth-century heiress, who by marrying into the Edgcumbe family brought the ownership of Stonehouse and Maker into their hands. Emma Place was named after Lady Emma Edgcumbe, and Caroline Place was named after her sister Lady Caroline Edgcumbe. The grand houses built in the area were, at one time, inhabited by the rich and successful.

At the far end of Durnford Street is the Anglican Church of St Paul. It was designed by John Foulston and was opened in 1831. When the Church of St George was destroyed in the Second World War, the two parishes were combined.

Branching off further along on the right is Admirals Hard. Regular ferries leave from the jetty and take passengers over to Cremyll on the Mount Edgcumbe estate.

The grand houses at Durnford Street.

E

Efford Cemetery

Efford Cemetery was laid out in 1904 and opened in 1907, initially covering 37 acres. There are 338 scattered Commonwealth war graves of First World War servicemen, including ten of New Zealand soldiers who were killed by the Bere Ferrers rail accident in 1917. There are also eight members of the Chinese Labour Corps – the largest amount buried in England.

After the heavy bombing over the two nights of 20 and 21 March 1941, naval ratings from HMS *Raleigh* were given the grim task of recovering the 292 bodies from the ruins, which were later buried in a mass grave at Efford cemetery. Lord Astor requested that if he was killed during enemy action he should have no special ceremony and should be buried alongside his fellow Plymothians.

The graveyard also contains reburials from disused burial grounds at Charles Street Quaker Burial Ground, St Andrew's Church and Charles Church.

A mass burial of the victims of the Blitz at Efford Cemetery.

Egyptian House

The Odd Fellows Hall can be found at the top of Ker Street, near the Devonport Column and Guildhall. It was designed by John Foulston and was built in 1823. At that time, it was more popularly known as the Egyptian House. There is another similar Egyptian-style house in Penzance that has three floors, whereas the one in Devonport only has two. On the front of the building is a plaque that reads: 'EGYPTIAN HOUSE. Designed in the Egyptian style following the popularisation of Egyptian architecture after the Napoleonic campaigns. One of only two such examples in the country. JOHN FOULSTON 1823.'

The first occupier of the building was the Stonehouse and Devonport Classical and Mathematical Subscription School. In 1827, the building was bought by the Civil and Military Library who opened it as a public library and newsroom. In 1867, it was sold to the Odd Fellows Society who, for a time, leased it to the Mount Zion Congregation. However, the building stayed in the hands of the Odd Fellows for almost 100 years before being purchased in 1968 by Tony Cooper, the owner of the nearby Forum in Fore Street, who turned it into a social club.

The Egyptian House at Ker Street, Devonport.

Elizabethan House

In 1584, the Mayor of Plymouth, John Sperkes, approved the building of New Street to house people who made their livelihood in and around the harbour. William Hele was one of the earliest recorded occupants in 1631. He had previously bought the dwelling from a merchant called Richard Brendan for £150.

In 1746, the London Company of Merchant Ventures were based in New Street while their associates developed and explored the fishing grounds of Newfoundland.

At the beginning of the twentieth century, the Addison Housing Act identified nineteen different areas of Plymouth, which it suggested should be cleared including the Elizabethan quarters. In 1929, the final occupant of the Elizabethan House handed over his deeds to the council for a demolition fee. Local MPs, however, called for some buildings within the city to be saved and reconditioned and the cause was supported by the Old Plymouth Society. This resulted in No. 32 New Street being restored for the purpose of being either a Drake or Elizabethan Museum. Soon after it was handed over to the care and charge of the Museum Committee of the Plymouth Corporation.

The house is open to the public and also includes an interesting Elizabethan garden.

The Elizabethan House at New Street on the Barbican.

Elliot Terrace

Elliot Terrace was built in 1860 by John Pethick who was a respected builder and later mayor of the city between 1898 and 1900. Known as 'Honest John', he also built the Grand Hotel in 1879 and became its first owner. At the time the Grand was the only hotel in Plymouth with a sea view; adverts stated that it had the finest view in Europe.

In 1908, No. 3 Elliot Terrace was bought by Waldorf Astor who had come to Plymouth as a Unionist Parliamentary candidate, going on to become Mayor of Plymouth between 1939 and 1944. His wife Nancy later gave No. 3 Elliot Terrace to the city as a residence for future Lord Mayors.

Elliot Terrace, home of the Astors, on Plymouth Hoe.

F

Fisher's Nose Blockhouse

Fisher's Nose Blockhouse, located below the Citadel, was built in the late 1400s and was rearmed and modified during the time of Henry VIII to protect the area from attack from the sea. Also known as Lambhay Point Tower, it was incorporated into the design of Drake's Fort when the building was constructed in 1595 and left when that fort was later replaced by the Citadel. In 1716, the defence was renamed Queen Elizabeth Tower. It was also an air-raid shelter during the Second World War. Today it is used by the Royal Plymouth Corinthian Yacht Club.

Henry VIII was responsible for the building of several blockhouses, each defending the entry to Plymouth Sound. These included the ones at Mount Edgcumbe, Devil's Point, Firestone Bay, Millbay West and Millbay East.

Fisher's Nose Blockhouse with the Royal Citadel in the background.

Fore Street

Fore Street in Devonport was once a busy shopping area before it was heavily bombed during the Second World War. Over 100 businesses lined the street from Granby Barracks to the dock gates. These included Woolworths, Timothy Whites, Liptons and Marks & Spencer's. Cinemas included the Electric Cinema and the Forum as well as the Tivoli, which stood at No. 8 Fore Street. It was so named because the design of the nearby post office was copied from the Tivoli in Rome. The ornate post office was decorated with symbols of postal dispatch and the produce of England. During the Second World War, the Local Defence Volunteers, who would later become the Home Guard, defended the post office during the night hours. The six men on patrol had a rifle each, but only one clip of ammunition. The Two Trees stood at No. 85 and beside it was Bateman Opticians. Other shops included Singers and David Greig as well as Aggie Weston's. All that remains today is the Forum Cinema, which is now a bingo hall.

The Forum at Fore Street, Devonport.

The recently rebuilt Fore Street, which includes the old Midland Bank building.

Freedom Fields

Freedom Park was given its name after the defeat of the French in 1403. Mock battles were re-enacted at the park by local children remembering the times when locals fought off the invading Bretons.

Freedom Park was the scene of a great battle on 3 December 1643 when the Roundheads fought off the Cavalier forces. A monument in the park marks the action and a plaque reads:

> Upon this spot on Sunday 3 December 1643, after hard fighting for several hours, the Roundhead garrison of Plymouth made their final rally and routed the Cavalier army which had surprised the outworks and well nigh taken the town. For many years it was the custom to celebrate the anniversary of this victory, long known as 'The Sabbath Day Fight', and recorded as 'The Great Deliverance' of the protracted siege, successfully sustained by troops and townsfolk on behalf of the Parliament against the King under great hardships for more than three years.

Furneaux, Captain Tobias

Tobias Furneaux was born at Swilly House in 1735. He was the son of William Furneaux (1696–1748) of Swilly and Susanna Wilcocks (1698–1775).

He joined the Royal Navy and served on the French and African coasts and in the West Indies towards the latter part of the Seven Years' War (1760–63). He became second lieutenant on board HMS *Dolphin* under Captain Samuel Wallis on a voyage around the world during 1766 to 1768. Furneaux became the first English man to set foot on Tahiti after Wallis became sick and was confined to his cabin, claiming the land in the name of His Majesty on 25 June 1767.

During November 1771, Furneaux commanded HMS *Adventure*, accompanying James Cook, sailing in *Resolution*, on his second voyage of exploration. He was the first man to circumnavigate the world both ways and the first British man to chart Tasmania and step foot there in 1773.

Furneaux died unmarried, aged forty-six, in 1781 and was buried in Stoke Damerel Church.

Gilbert, Humphrey

Sir Humphrey Gilbert was born in Compton in 1539 and became an adventurer, explorer, Member of Parliament and soldier, serving during the reign of Elizabeth I. He was the half-brother of Sir Walter Raleigh and the cousin of Sir Richard Grenville. At Oxford he studied navigation and military science before joining the army, and later in 1563 was wounded at the siege of Le Havre. He put down an uprising in Ireland for which he was knighted.

A portrait of Sir Humphrey Gilbert.

On 11 June 1583, he sailed from Plymouth arriving at St John's, Newfoundland, on 3 August, claiming the land in the name of the queen. On 29 August of the same year, he headed south with three ships but lost the largest of them before turning homeward two days later. The last sighting of Gilbert was during a violent storm in the Atlantic before his ship was swallowed by the sea, resulting in his death aged forty-four.

Gin Distillery

The Plymouth Gin Distillery is the oldest working distillery in England and has been making Plymouth Gin since 1793.

The building on the Barbican dates from the early 1400s. The Refectory Room was once a medieval hall and features a fine hull-shaped timber roof, built in 1431. It was formally a monastery, occupied by the Black Friars, until the Reformation and Dissolution of the Monasteries. It later became Plymouth's debtor's prison.

In 1620, the Pilgrim Fathers spent their last night there before setting sail on the *Mayflower* to start a new life in America. Today, the *Mayflower* appears on the label of every bottle of Plymouth Gin produced.

Records show that Black Friars was used as a 'mault-house' as far back as 1697, although the distilling of Plymouth Gin only started in 1793 when Mr Coates joined the established distilling business of Fox & Williamson.

Above left: The Gin Distillery at Southside Street on the Barbican.

Above right: The Plymouth Gin tower rising above the distillery.

Golden Hind

The *Golden Hind* was a galleon captained by Sir Francis Drake when he circumnavigated the world between 1577 and 1580. The ship was originally known as *Pelican*; however, Drake renamed the vessel mid-voyage in 1578 in honour of one of the principal sponsors, Sir Christopher Hatton, whose crest was a golden hind.

Elizabeth I partly sponsored Drake to lead an expedition, sailing around South America through the Strait of Magellan and exploring the coast beyond. Drake, however, with the unofficial support of Queen Elizabeth, acted as a privateer. In December 1577 he set sail with five small ships, crewed with 164 men, reaching the Brazilian coast in early 1578.

On 1 March 1579, the *Golden Hind* captured the Spanish galleon *Nuestra Señora de la Concepción* off the coast of Ecuador. This galleon contained the largest treasure captured to date, including over 360,000 pesos – equivalent to almost £500 million today. The haul took six days to transport and included 26 tons of silver and half a ton of gold, as well as porcelain, jewellery, coins, and jewels.

On 26 September 1580, Drake sailed into Plymouth Harbour with fifty-six of the original eighty crew left aboard. The vessel was unloaded at Trematon Castle, supervised by the queen's guards. The treasure included 6 tons of cloves from the Spice Islands, which were highly valuable – at the time worth their weight in gold. Over half of the proceeds went to the queen and were used to pay off the annual debt.

After Drake's circumnavigation the *Golden Hind* was put on public exhibition at the dockyard at Deptford, London, remaining there from 1580 to around 1650 when it fell into disrepair and was broken up.

A portrait of Sir Francis Drake. (Courtesy of the Library of Congress)

Guildhall

The Guildhall was built between 1870 and 1874 at a cost of £50,000. It was almost completely destroyed during the Blitz (1941) when only its outer shell remained. It was originally built by a local man, John Pethick, who later became mayor in 1898.

   The great hall, which was 146 feet by 58 feet, was totally destroyed by the bombing of 1941 and it took another ten years to decide whether to rebuild or demolish it completely. It was finally decided to rebuild it and it was reopened in 1959, some eighteen years later.

The Guildhall with Royal Parade in the background.

Hardy, Sir Thomas Masterman

No. 156 Durnford Street is the house where Vice-Admiral Sir Thomas Masterman Hardy once lived. A plaque marks the spot. Although he rose through the ranks to become a vice admiral, his naval career is remembered by just three words: 'Kiss me Hardy'. When Vice Admiral Horatio Nelson was fatally wounded aboard HMS *Victory* in 1805, he was taken below deck where he was later visited by Hardy. Nelson's words to him were, 'Take care of poor Lady Hamilton', before he uttered the immortal words, 'kiss me, Hardy'. It has been suggested that what Nelson actually said was 'Kismet, Hardy,' meaning that this was his fate. However, that was not the case as many officers present, including his surgeon William Beatty who wrote

The house where
Sir Thomas Masterman
Hardy once lived.

down his words, bore witness to the actual event. When Nelson uttered the words 'kiss me, Hardy', Hardy knelt beside him and kissed him on the cheek. Many people think that these were his last words, but his final words were uttered just before he died, three hours after he had been shot. These words were 'God and my country'.

A young sailor from Cawsand, Lieutenant John Pollard, was a midshipman on the *Victory* when Nelson was fatally wounded. Although not a well-known name now, it was Pollard who shot and killed the enemy sailor who shot Nelson. He was known thereafter as 'Nelson's Avenger'. However, several other men also claimed to have shot the Frenchman.

Hawkins, John

In 1562, England's involvement in slavery began in Plymouth when John Hawkins sailed from the Barbican with three ships and kidnapped 400 Africans in Guinea before taking them to the West Indies to trade. Between 1562 and 1567, he and his cousin, Francis Drake, made three voyages to Guinea and Sierra Leone, enslaving a total of almost 1,400 Africans. Slavers' records from that time show that probably more than three times that amount of Africans died during the exercise.

Hawkins made so much money from the practice that Elizabeth I granted him a special coat of arms. In 1577, he was made treasurer for the navy and was knighted in 1588 by the Lord High Admiral, Charles Howard, after the fall of the Spanish Armada.

Hawkins died on 12 November 1595 after becoming sick on a treasure-hunting voyage with Francis Drake in the West Indies. Drake also died of the sickness, probably dysentery, on 27 January and was buried at sea.

John Hawkins.

Higher St Budeaux Church

In AD 480 Budoc, the Bishop of Dol, sailed across from Brittany to the southern English coast and landed his craft in an inlet off the River Tamar. This inlet is believed to be at Tamerton Creek. A crude stone cross was erected by him in Ernesettle Woods and a chapel was built near to Warren Point. The original building was just a small wattle church, but later a permanent stone church was built, just before the Norman invasion, and was dedicated to Budoc.

In the early Tudor period there were demands for a bigger church to be built at St Budeaux. It was completed in 1563 – five years into the reign of Elizabeth I.

In 1569, the church saw the marriage of Sir Francis Drake and Mary Newman.

During the Civil War, Plymouth and its surrounding villages such as St Budeaux had sworn an oath to fight and die for the Parliamentarian cause. Those who did not comply faced hanging. However, in Cornwall the people supported the Royalist cause and made raids across the water on parts of St Budeaux. For a time the church at Higher St Budeaux was used as a garrison by the Royalists. On 16 April 1644, Lieutenant Colonel Martin, who commanded the Parliamentarian garrison at Plymouth, sent 600 musketeers with 120 horses to attack the 500 Cavaliers stationed at St Budeaux. Because of a mistake made by guides, the horses went one way and the

The church at Higher St Budeaux.

attacking party went another. Nevertheless, the foot soldiers arrived at the church and, not being expected, saw off the enemy and captured the church tower. Altogether they captured two officers and forty-four other prisoners. They also took three barrels of gunpowder, twenty horses and around twenty arms. It was said that most of the prisoners then joined the Parliamentarian forces.

On 27 December 1644, St Budeaux was again the scene of much bloodshed. The Roundheads marched from Kinterbury towards the church, which was now a garrison for the Parliamentarians, and fought for an hour and a half before the church was recaptured. The Royalists also captured Major Stucley, together with twenty officers and 100 soldiers. Ten of the defenders were killed as were seven of the Roundheads including Major Haynes. A mound in a garden at Plaistow Hill, near the church, is said to be the place where those who died in the battle were buried.

During the siege of Plymouth by the Royalists, the inhabitants of St Budeaux took provisions into town for the men and their horses. Prince Maurice issued a warrant that stated: 'To the constables or tythingmen of Saint Budeaux and Pennycross, threatening proceedings against all who should carry with him horse, oxen or kine, or sheep or other provision for men or horse into the said town of Plymouth for the relief of the rebells there.' After the battle, the church was little more than a wreck, and it wasn't restored until 1655.

Hoe

The Hoe, or 'Hoh' as it was once called, means the spur of a hill or a high place. The Hoe has been a popular gathering place for hundreds of years. It is steeped in history. From ancient times limestone drawings of the giants Gog and Magog were cut into the grass on the Hoe. They would have been there when Francis Drake played his much written about game of bowls as he got word of the Armada approaching. During the time that Francis Drake was mayor, a mariner's compass was newly erected on the Hoe on Wynderygge Hill. It survived until 1730.

The Hoe witnessed the Civil War in the 1640s and the building of the Citadel in the 1660s. A windmill once stood on the top of the Hoe, and this is shown on a Civil War map of 1643. It was reported that its vane was shot off during an attack from the fort at Mount Batten. Another landmark on the Hoe was the Trinity Obelisk, which was destroyed in 1882. The triangular obelisk served as a navigation marker for ships in the Sound. Workmen removed the obelisk under the direction of John Pethick, a local contractor. Crowds gathered around to see the obelisk blown apart by gunpowder on 18 October 1882. The reason that it was destroyed was because two days later, on 20 October 1882, the foundation stone for Smeaton's Tower was laid in its place.

For many years the Hoe was just rough grass where sheep and cows grazed. In the 1880s, the Hoe took on its present layout when new paths, grassed areas and monuments were laid out. At the same time the Hoe area was generally tidied up.

Plymouth Hoe, looking towards the Lido and Smeaton's Tower.

Some of the present-day buildings and monuments that were erected during the late 1800s include the Marine Biological Association's Aquarium, The Belvedere, Drake's statue, the National Armada Memorial, Norrington's Fountain and, of course, Smeaton's Tower. Other attractions during the Victorian period included the Camera Obscura, the bandstand and the Promenade Pier.

For hundreds of years the Hoe has attracted many thousands of people who have gathered for various events. In 1625, 10,000 troops paraded here during a visit by Charles I and his queen. Executions also drew large crowds, especially when three young marines met death by firing squad in 1797.

In 1815, people gathered on the Hoe to see the captured Napoleon on the deck of the ship *Bellerphon*. When the Prince of Wales married in 1863, 5,000 children sang in unison on the Hoe. In 1967, thousands of people waited on the Hoe for the return of Sir Francis Chichester after his single-handed voyage.

Between the wars the Tinside Lido was built, together with the limestone-fronted bathing houses, the terraces and the changing rooms. The cliff paths towards the foreshore were built and electric lighting was installed around the bathing area in 1932.

During the war years the Hoe proved again to be a very popular meeting place as people danced on the promenade on warm evenings in defiance of the German bombing. The Promenade Pier was bombed and destroyed during 1941.

I

Island House

The Island House on the Barbican was built between 1572 and 1600 and was one of the houses that the Pilgrim Fathers stayed at before leaving on the *Mayflower* for America in 1620.

Robert Bayly and his wife Hannah leased the Island House from Sir William Molesworth in the early 1700s. Their son John moved to Plymouth in 1737 and joined Captain Brabant in his merchants and shipowning business. When Brabant died in 1763 the business passed to John Bayly, and in 1786 he purchased the freehold of Island House from Sir William Molesworth.

Island House stayed in the possession of the Bayly family until Mrs Emma Sophia Bayly died in 1924. She was the widow of Robert Bayly (1839–1901) who lived at Torr House, Pennycross, Plymouth. Elizabeth Mary Bayly (1870–1958) repurchased the house and in 1935 gave it to her nephew, John, to look after.

The Strand Tea Rooms with the Island House on the right of the photo.

During enemy bombing on the night of 13 January 1941, the house suffered major damage. In 1948, John Bayley had the house restored by Messrs A. S. Parker and Allen. On 11 April 1949, Island House was officially reopened by the Lord Mayor of Plymouth before it was leased to Messrs S. J. Lethbridge.

It has had many uses over the years, more recently being used as a tourist information centre and a shop selling ice cream.

Above: A view of the Barbican and the Island House.

Left: A plaque on the side of the Island House commemorating the stay of the Pilgrim Fathers there in 1620.

J

Jacka Bakery

Jacka Bakery at No. 38 Southside Street is the oldest bakery in the country, dating back to the sixteenth century. The bakery was owned by the Fownes family in 1596 when wheat was 30s a bushell. The bakery was there when Francis Drake, John Hawkins and Walter Raleigh lived nearby, and they could have well visited the establishment. It is said that the Pilgrim Fathers took biscuits baked at Jacka's on their journey when they set sail for America in the *Mayflower* in 1620.

In the early 1900s the bakery was owned by F. F. Warren and staff included his wife Kate.

In the Second World War, families were allowed to use the ovens at Jacka's to cook their dinners.

Today, under new ownership, the bakery is as popular as it has ever been.

An older shot of the shopfront of F. H. Jacka's bakery on the Barbican showing how it once looked before the recent renovation.

Ker Street

Ker Street, stretching from Monument Street to George Street, was the formal approach to the Devonport Acropolis, which consisted of John Foulston's Odd Fellowes Hall (1823), built in the Egyptian style; the Zion Chapel, in Islamic style complete with minarets; the Guildhall (1821) in Greek Doric style, copying the Parthenon; and the Column (1824) in Doric style and built from Cornish granite.

In 1746, John Wesley preached there and a chapel was erected twenty years later, although it was demolished in 1941.

Until the early 1800s, the area was known as Windmill Hill. Terraced houses were built in Ker Street in the 1820s but were damaged during the Blitz. Some properties survived until they were demolished in the 1960s and these were replaced with poorly planned blocks of flats. Today the old flats are gone and modern dwellings stand in their place.

The Guildhall and Column at Ker Street, Devonport.

The approach to the Guildhall at Ker Street.

Children playing among the debris in Ker Street soon after the Second World War.

Keyham Station

Keyham station was opened in 1900 by the Great Western Railway. It was once well used, particularly by the men of the nearby Royal Naval Barracks, which was originally known as HMS *Vivid* but was later renamed HMS *Drake* in 1934. Today, although the station remains open, it is unstaffed and eerily quiet at the best of times; the shelters and waiting room are long gone.

Keyham station close to the naval base at HMS *Drake*.

King Street

King Street once ran from Cambridge Street to Stoke Road and Manor Street. In the early part of the 1900s, hawkers and entertainers gathered underneath the arch. One was Mr Pratt who, with his monkey Bruce, entertained passersby while playing his organ grinder. Bruce wore a red hat and jacket and was well known to the people living in the area. Mr Pratt, his wife and his monkey all lived in one tiny room in the street. Small audiences would gather to watch Bruce and would feed him chipped potatoes, which were sold in the evening by Italians living in the area (by day, they would sell ice cream around the town from their small handcarts). Another well-known figure was a blind Cornish miner who sold boot and shoe laces that were draped from his left arm while, with his right hand, he would hold out a tin cup to collect money.

Many beerhouses sprung up in the area during the 1850s, including The Thistle Rose and Shamrock, The Hen and Chicken and The Botanic Garden which was near Flora Street Nursery. In the shadow of the railway embankment stood The Robert Burns, The Broad Gauge and The Tandem Inn.

As a barrel organ played, bruised fruit was sold at knock-down prices and women gathered to attend late night auctions selling cheap cuts of meat. Chestnut sellers would also ply their trade from a warm fire and a man on stilts would tap on windows to announce forthcoming events such as the fair or the circus. Rabbit formed a staple part of people's diet and a rabbit catcher with four or five rabbits hanging from his arm would sell and skin the creatures on the spot.

Perhaps one of the best-remembered outlets in King Street was Ivor Dewdney's pasty shop, which was at No. 2 and opened in the 1930s.

Torn apart in the Second World War, the area has seen a lot of changes and rebuilding over the years. When the arch was pulled down in the 1970s a major part of the street disappeared, and the hawkers and entertainers of past years were soon forgotten.

King Street approaching Frankfort Gate.

Laurel and Hardy

Laurel and Hardy appeared at the Palace Theatre on 17 May 1954. Stan and Ollie were touring the country, appearing in a show called *Birds of a Feather*. The shows in Plymouth were to have been their last shows of the tour. Playing on the same bill at the time were Harry Worth and 'Wonder Horse Tony'. Unfortunately, Oliver Hardy had a severe bout of the flu and also had a mild heart attack, so the show was cancelled. Ollie spent the rest of his stay in Plymouth recovering at the Grand Hotel on the Hoe.

An advert for Laurel and Hardy's appearance at the Palace Theatre.

The brass plaque commemorating Laurel and Hardy outside the theatre in Union Street.

Laurel and Hardy had visited Britain once before in 1932 when they were mobbed wherever they went. When they returned in 1954 they were handicapped by age and illness but still managed to give an exhausting thirteen shows a week. After they had to cancel the show, Stan Laurel wrote a letter to the manager of the Palace Theatre, William Willis, apologising. It read:

My Dear Mr Willis,

Please pardon delay in acknowledgement of your kind letter of the 22nd.inst. which was deeply appreciated. Many many thanks.

Mr Hardy is feeling better but, of course, is still very weak. However, we are sailing for the States on June 2nd, so I think the voyage and rest will do him a lot of good.

We too were very much disappointed, not being able to fulfil our engagement with you – unfortunate for all concerned, could have been a profitable and happy week. Anyway, we hope to have the opportunity and pleasure of meeting and playing for you again in the near future.

Mrs Laurel and Mr and Mrs Hardy join in kindest regards and every good wish always, and remember us kindly to Mr Heath, the staff and regular patrons.

Very Sincerely:

Stan Laurel.

Lido

The Lido was designed by S. Wibberley, a city engineer who also designed the surrounding buildings built into the cliffside. It featured a classic semicircle swimming area together with three fountains cascading water into the pool. The water was drawn from the sea and pumped through the cascades to give a complete change of water every four hours.

The Lido at Plymouth Hoe.

Looking across the Lido towards Plymouth Sound.

The Lido was officially opened on 2 October 1935 by the Lord Mayor, Lieutenant-Commander E. W. Rogers. The three fountains were floodlit at night and gave three different colour changes.

Art deco in style, in its heyday it was a glorious sight. It was described in 1935 as 'one of the finest open-sea bathing centres in the country'. Orchestras played above in the terraces as people swam. It was also once a popular venue for beauty contests.

During the war years, people used the Lido to wash in after spending many hours clearing up the bomb-ravaged streets of Plymouth. Unfortunately, the distinctive shape of the pool helped German bombers get their bearings as they flew towards the city during their many raids.

Today the pool has been restored and during the summer months is well used, but is not quite as popular as it had been in previous decades.

Liners

Plymothians would line the docks in the hope of seeing famous passengers disembark from the many ocean liners that called at Millbay. The *Queen Mary* was Cunard's pride and joy. Famous passengers who docked at Plymouth on the vessel included Gloria Swanson and Jack Warner, who both arrived in the city in 1938.

The *Mauretania* came to Plymouth regularly and delivered passengers and mail to the city. Film stars were quite often among the passengers, including the American crooner Bing Crosby. The *Mauretania* was built by Swan, Hunter and Wigham in Newcastle in 1907 and was the world's fastest liner from 1907 to 1927 and was part of Cunard Line's Liverpool to New York service.

Charlie Chaplin disembarked from the *Mauretania* in 1931 to the delight of the many Plymothians who had come to see him. Thousands of people gathered in the streets to catch a glimpse of the celebrity. The star of many silent films, he made his famous film *City Lights* in the same year. While in Plymouth, Chaplin was the guest of Nancy Astor at her home in Elliott Terrace on the Hoe. Also visiting Astor at the same time were Amy Johnson and George Bernard Shaw. The *Mauretania* made its final eastwards crossing on September 1934 – from New York to Southampton – and was sent to the breakers yard in July 1935.

The *Normandie* steamed into Plymouth Sound in 1937 after crossing the Atlantic in a record-breaking time. The *Normandie* was the industry's first 1,000-foot ocean liner. Walt Disney was among the many famous passengers who landed at Plymouth. The liner capsized and caught fire in New York while being converted for use in the Second World War.

Liner passengers continued their onward journeys to London from Millbay station. The station and nearby hotels were built to accommodate the endless stream of visitors.

The days of the great ocean liners calling at Plymouth with celebrity guests are now long gone, but occasionally one drops anchor in the Sound, although they are few and far between.

A plaque on the approach towards Millbay Docks marking the arrival of Bing Crosby by liner to Plymouth.

Millbay Docks where many famous people disembarked from the numerous liners that once visited the city.

Lockyer Street

The philatelist Stanley Gibbons lived at No. 8 Lockyer Street from 1872 where he also ran his business dealing in stamps.

What is now the Invicta Hotel was built during the reign of Queen Victoria by William Phillips and designed by George Wightwick, who worked with Plymouth's leading architect John Foulston. Originally, the building was two separate merchant houses. During the bombing of 1941, the properties were severely damaged. Reginald George Hyett, the owner of one of the buildings (a hotel), was killed during the raid.

The Hyett family had owned both properties since 1890 and decided to bring both buildings together as one business, which they called the Osborne Hotel. The hotel was later renamed the Invicta in 1952.

Nearby, the Royal Hotel adjoined the Theatre Royal in George Street. Work was started on the building in 1811 from plans drawn up by John Foulston. It took two years to complete at a cost of £60,000. A casualty of the Blitz, the site was occupied for many years after by a small car park. Opposite the Royal Hotel stood the Lockyer Hotel. The Devon and Cornwall Female Orphanage on the corner of Lockyer Street and Citadel Road was also badly damaged during the Second World War.

Lockyer Street looking towards the city centre.

Looe Street

At one time, Sir Francis Drake lived at Looe Street before moving to Buckland Abbey. The name of the street is said to have arisen from the fact that swine once ran loose there. It was also once known as Pike Street and housed the town's chief hotel, the Pope's Head. Dr Johnston stayed there in 1762 whilst on his travels.

The Minerva, at No. 31 Looe Street, is Plymouth's oldest public house, dating from 1540. During the 1600s the pub was home to press gangs who would drop the king's shilling into potential sailors' pints of ale. The men unwittingly accepted the payment and were led off to serve on various naval vessels. Some of the timber used in the pub is said to have come from the Spanish Armada, although the fleet didn't set sale until 1588 so would have had to have been added at a later date.

The inn also boasts several ghosts spotted by many landlords and visitors over the years.

Between 1861 and 1970, the owners of the establishment were the Octagon Brewery, who traded at Martin Street.

Above left: The plaque above a dwelling at the top of Looe Street celebrating that Sir Francis Drake once lived there.

Above right: An early photo showing Looe Street and some of its residents.

Below: Looking down Looe Street towards the Barbican.

M

Merchant's House

Originally built as a wealthy merchant's house in the 1600s, this replaced an earlier house that stood on the same spot in the 1500s. At least three mayors lived here, including its first owner William Parker.

At one time the house was used as a taxi office. After falling into disrepair, Plymouth City Council bought the house in 1972, restoring it to its former glory.

Park's chemist was originally situated on Mutley Plain and later the contents were displayed in the apothecary room at the Merchant's House, located at St Andrew's Street. Other displays at the house over the years have included ones relating to Plymouth's past history, transport, Victorian exhibits, as well as items relating to the Second World War and the Blitz.

The Merchant's House on the approach to the Barbican.

A view of Millbay Docks and Plymouth Hoe.

Millbay Docks

The docks were designed by Isambard Kingdom Brunel, and Millbay was linked to the railway in 1849. The docks soon became a port of call for the Irish Steamship Company and Brunel's services were further engaged for the construction of an extra pier to hold 4,000 tons of coal. The docks became one of the main coaling stations in the English Channel.

Many marine and engineering businesses set up nearby to the docks to service the many vessels belonging to the Royal Mail Steamship Company, the War Department, HM Customs and many others.

Passenger numbers grew and many luxury liners called at the docks. As well as regular passengers, as previously mentioned, there were many celebrities that disembarked at Millbay. These included John F. Kennedy, John Wayne, General Allenby, Maurice Chevalier, Winston Churchill, Clemenceau, Bebe Daniels, Marlene Dietrich, Douglas Fairbanks, Helen Keller, Pierre Laval, Vivian Leigh, Lloyd George, Ben Lyon, Anna Pavlova, General Pershing, Mary Pickford, Cecil Rhodes, Bernard Shaw, General Smuts and H. G. Wells.

Millbridge

In 1525, Sir Piers Edgcumbe was responsible for building Millbridge as well as the corn mills found there. In around 1884 it was decided to fill in the upper part of Stonehouse Creek, known as the 'Deadlake'. It formed part of the millpond for Stonehouse Mill. The Deadlake had become a health hazard and a petition was organised that was then put to the three local authorities of Plymouth, Devonport and Stonehouse, who agreed to purchase it from the Earl of Mount Edgcumbe in 1890. In 1895, 400 tons of rubble was used to fill the Deadlake. Some of it came from the old tram depot at Compton, although much of the rubble came from the quarries at Cattedown and Oreston. The area was reopened in 1898 as Victoria Park.

The road
through
Millbridge
looking
towards
Victoria Park.

Mount Batten

There's evidence that the earliest trade with Europe took place at Mount Batten in the late Bronze Age. Trade continued throughout the Iron Age period and into the Roman period. Ancient finds along the peninsula include three British-made bronze mirrors as well as many other items; unfortunately, these were all destroyed in the Blitz.

T. E. Lawrence was stationed at Mount Batten in Plymouth, being posted to RAF *Cattewater* during March 1929. He stayed in Plymouth until 1935 where he worked on high-speed boats.

Previously, at the beginning of the First World War Lawrence had been a university post-graduate researcher and had travelled extensively within the Ottoman Empire.

The tower
at Mount
Batten.

The Pier at Mount Batten stretching out towards Plymouth Sound.

When he volunteered his services, he was posted to Cairo. Lawrence fought with the Arab troops against the enemy forces of the empire. In 1918, he was involved in the capture of Damascus and was promoted to lieutenant colonel. After the war his fame spread and he became known as 'Lawrence of Arabia'.

When he joined the RAF in 1922, he enlisted as John Hume Ross to protect his identity. This was discovered in 1923 and he was forced out of the RAF. He changed his name to T. E. Shaw and enlisted in the Royal Tank Corps. He was unhappy there and petitioned the RAF to reaccept him, which they did in 1925.

He died aged forty-six in a motorbike accident near his cottage in Wareham. There is a plaque at Turnchapel that commemorates Lawrence. It reads:

Lawrence of Arabia 1888–1935.
On his return from India in 1929, T. E. Lawrence, under the assumed name of Shaw, was posted to a flying boat squadron at RAF Mount Batten. He remained in the marine craft section until his discharge on 19 February 1935.

Mount Edgcumbe Training Ship

The *Mount Edgcumbe* industrial training ship was for homeless and destitute boys. The ship was recommissioned as a training ship in 1877. It was moored off Saltash Passage, but when cables were laid to the north of the Royal Albert Bridge in 1913, it was moved to the Saltash side.

Goshawk, a seagoing training vessel, was moored nearby. At the time, Herbert Price Knevitt was the superintendent captain. He was retired from the navy and lived on board with his wife Isabella and their three daughters, Nellie, Nora and Ella. He was forty-seven at the time and his wife was thirty-five. They also had a servant, Louise Chapman, who was twenty-six, who cooked and kept their quarters tidy. There were also three instructors, the oldest being sixty-two and the youngest being thirty-four, and a schoolmaster, James Sale Gitsham, who was twenty-seven. Everyone else on board was referred to as 'inmates' and were all aged between twelve and sixteen. Some came from Plymouth but they also came from other parts of the country, from London to the Isle of Wight.

It wasn't difficult for the boys to find themselves on a training ship. A law in 1884 said that the qualifications for being on the boat were:

> Anyone found begging or receiving alms, anyone found wandering who doesn't have a proper home, proper guardianship or means to support themselves, anyone found destitute or who is an orphan or who has a surviving parent who is in prison, anyone who frequents the company of thieves or any child that a parent feels is uncontrollable. No boys who have been in prison are allowed on the boat and the payment required for residence is 8s a week.

In 1910, Captain H. Wesley Harkcom took over the ship and changed the way it had been run for many years. He stopped using the birch on the boys, he moved his family on board, and he bought many of the provisions needed from local dealers, including food from the Saltash Co-op and coal from Ware's of Saltash Passage. Harkcom was an expert in rowing and encouraged the boys to take up this pastime. The ship also had a brass band and they gave concerts on the green at St Budeaux and in the nearby parish church. There was said to be anything up to 250 boys on the ship at one time and many went on to see service in the navy.

On 4 December 1920, the training ship was closed down and was sold on 18 April 1921 before being broken up at Queen Anne's Battery.

The area of the River Tamar where the *Mount Edgcumbe* Training Ship was once moored.

New Street

New Street on the Barbican was at one time known as Greyfriars Street and later Rag Lane. It was once the site of a fourteenth-century Franciscan friary, which was demolished in the 1530s after Henry VIII's Dissolution of the Monasteries. Local merchant and businessman John Sparke laid out the street as we know it today in the early sixteenth century, and in 1584 it was recorded as 'Sparke's Newe Street'. Sparke was the first Englishman to use and document the words potatoes and tobacco, both names originating from South America.

Elizabethan dwellings and warehouses fronted onto the narrow lane, their large backyards consisting of a network of alleys.

Until the 1840s Sutton Harbour was the main commercial port in Plymouth, but by the mid-nineteenth century New Street's fortunes had diminished. Towards the end of the 1800s New Street became very overcrowded, becoming a slum, with up to twenty-four people living in one property. At the time diseases including smallpox, diphtheria and scarlet fever were commonplace.

New Street on the Barbican.

Normandy Landings

In January 1944, the US army set up camp at Vicarage Road, St Budeaux, in preparation for the D-Day landings. Altogether the camp housed 60,000 troops. The whole operation was top secret, and from May 1944 anyone who wanted to visit relatives in the area had to apply for a permit and were escorted to the address by military police. They also had to give a specific time when they would be leaving. During this period the river was full of ships loading men and equipment. Children in the area loved the American troops and pestered them for sweets, chewing gum, chocolate, food and cocoa, etc. The Americans weren't affected by rationing and were very generous to the locals, especially the children. In the city, they even organised parties for them.

The large majority of troops in Plymouth were from the 29th Armoured Division. Residents remember that the area was a hive of activity while the troops were there, but awoke one morning to find that they'd all gone, leaving just a baseball bat behind. The Vicarage Road camp was decommissioned in September 1945.

After the war Tamar Terrace was renamed Normandy Way and Vicarage Road was renamed Normandy Hill to commemorate the many troops who passed by that way. A memorial was later erected in the gardens and the plaque upon it reads:

This tablet marks the departure from this place of units of the V and V11 corps of the United States Army on the 6th June 1944 for the D-Day landings in France and was unveiled by His Excellency John Hay Whitney, the Ambassador of the United States of America.
May 1958.

Above: American troops leaving from Saltash Passage for D-Day.

Right: Normandy Way, St Budeaux, named after the many soldiers who left for D-Day from nearby Saltash Passage.

Notte Street

Notte Street, formerly a hazel grove, was originally called Nut Street. Sir Walter Raleigh reputedly lived at No. 12. The original building, which once had wooden carvings depicting the coats of arms of local merchants, was where Catherine of Aragon was entertained when she arrived in Plymouth in 1501. The house was totally reconstructed by the Bulteel family who added artisans' dwellings in 1883. The terrace, which was half-timbered, was demolished in 1963. Notte Street was also home to William Cookworthy (1705–80), who first discovered china clay at Tregonning Hill between Helston and Marazion.

Left: The view looking down Notte Street towards the Barbican.

Below: Notte Street heading towards Armada Way and showing the Civic Centre and the tower of the Guildhall.

O

Ocean Quay

Ocean Quay railway station, developed by the London and South West Railway, was used extensively by passengers disembarking from the many luxury liners that once called at Plymouth. It was also used for goods traffic until 1966.

Today, apartments stand at Ocean Quay complete with many impressive motor launches and yachts.

Ocean Quay with Royal William Yard in the background.

Old Town Street with the Drake Circus Shopping Centre in the distance.

Old Town Street

Old Town Street originally stretched from Spooner's Corner up to Tavistock Road. In the 1700s Plymouth consisted of just 1,600 houses – all around Sutton Harbour. The northern end of the town was where the top of Royal Parade is today, and Old Town Street led out into open countryside.

Old Town Street was continually widened over the years for ever-increasing forms of traffic. Before the war the street featured many well-known stores including Woolworths, Mumfords, La Brasseur and Notcutt the photographers.

Bombed extensively in the Second World War, the only part of the city that retains the name Old Town Street is by what was, for many years, the main post office at the top of Royal Parade, stretching towards New George Street.

Oreston

Oreston was originally a village on the southern bank of the Cattewater and was recorded as Horestone on a map of 1591. The name is thought to have derived from 'ores town' or 'Hora's tun' after a Saxon tenant farmer who held the lease before the Norman Conquest.

Oreston sided with the Royalists during the Civil War, and there was a battery there.

Alexander Selkirk married Frances Candish, a pub landlady, in Oreston in 1720 and lived in the village for a while. Selkirk was the inspiration for Daniel Defoe's book *Robinson Crusoe*.

In the early 1800s, the Admiralty Breakwater Quarries at Oreston breached caves and discovered fossil bones of prehistoric animals such as rhinos and lions. Stone from Oreston was used in the construction of Plymouth Breakwater, with the foundation stone being laid on Shovel Rock on 8 August 1812.

When the building of the fourth Eddystone Lighthouse, designed by James Douglass, began in 1879, Trinity House based their depot at Oreston. The light was first lit in 1882 and is still used today.

During the Second World War, the area suffered bomb damage but escaped the more severe destruction experienced by other parts of Plymouth.

P

Palace Theatre

The theatre in Union Street was originally called the New Palace Theatre of Varieties and was opened on 5 September 1898. The opening show featured Adele and May Lilian, who were billed as 'the Levey Sisters'. They performed Persian and hunting songs and were followed by an acrobatic act called the Six Craggs. Other acts that night included Walter and Edie Cassons who performed a vaudeville act, a comedian called Harry Comlin and a roller skater called Fred Darby. Tickets ranged from 1*s* to 2*s* 6*d*, which included three hours of entertainment.

Fire destroyed both the auditorium and stage on 23 December 1898, and the theatre wasn't opened again until May 1899.

There were twice-nightly vaudeville shows by 1902. Artists who appeared during the early 1900s included Neil Kenyon, billed as a 'Scotch' comedian; Robert Williams, a sword swinger; and Miss Gertie Gitana, who sang songs including 'Nellie Dean'.

Below left: The Palace Theatre in Union Street.

Below right: The ornate tower of the Palace Theatre.

In 1909, Harry Houdini played at the theatre for a week during August and drew a huge crowd. In 1931, Charlie Chaplin, who was in Plymouth as a guest of Nancy Astor, appeared on stage on 16 November of that year.

The theatre stayed open during the Blitz in 1941 to keep people's spirits up. Acts that appeared that year included Billy Cotton and his band, Tommy Handley, Arthur Lucan (Old Mother Riley), Henry Hall and his Orchestra as well as many lesser-known acts. At Christmas of that year, the main show was *Robinson Crusoe*, which starred George Hirstie.

The theatre closed in 1949 for redecorating and reopened with the Billy Cotton Bandshow. The theatre closed again in 1954 due to the lack of touring shows. It was offered to Plymouth City Council in 1956 but they refused to buy it and it closed for five months before reopening in October 1956. It closed suddenly on 7 February 1959 during the pantomime *Little Miss Muffet* because of lack of interest.

New management took over the theatre in 1961 and it became Palace Theatre (Bingo) Ltd. The theatre reopened in 1962 with the pantomime *Sinbad the Sailor*.

In 1965, Arthur Fox, a businessman from Manchester, paid £50,000 for the theatre with the intention of hosting Star Bingo, wrestling (which was very popular at the time) and striptease.

In 1975, it was bought by EMI and opened on 19 April 1977 with a performance of 'The Magic Flute'. The theatre struggled and closed on 27 May 1980 when it ceased trading and its contents were put up for sale. It reopened on 16 May 1981 for a review with Danny La Rue but finally closed in 1983 when it became the Academy Dance Hall. Its fortunes didn't improve, however, and today it remains closed with its shabby appearance hiding its varied history.

Pankhurst, Emmeline

Emmeline Pankhurst is best known as being the leader of the British suffragette movement, but her connection and arrest in Plymouth is perhaps lesser known.

Pankhurst was born in 1858. Her later political actions caused her to be arrested on many occasions. She founded the Women's Social and Political Union in 1898 and the group became infamous for smashing windows and assaulting policemen in their fight against political parties of the time. Pankhurst, her daughters and other WSPU activists were sentenced to repeated prison sentences. Her arrest in Plymouth was carried in the *Morning Post* of 5 December 1913:

Mrs. Pankhurst was arrested on board the White Star steamship Majestic on arrival at Plymouth yesterday about noon from New York, and was subsequently taken to Exeter Gaol by motor car in charge of a police officer and of detectives who had come from London. While at dinner on Wednesday evening she was informed of the action that the Government had decided to take, and when the Chief Constable of Plymouth,

Women's rights campaigner Emmeline Pankhurst.
(Courtesy of the Library of Congress)

two officers from Scotland Yard and others instructed for the arrest went on board the Majestic, Mrs. Pankhurst was asked to come to the Purser's office to see them. She refused to do so, and the police, going to the promenade deck, made the arrest in the presence of many of the passengers. There was no scene or demonstration. When the Chief Constable of Plymouth asked Mrs. Pankhurst to consider herself under arrest she demanded his authority, and was answered that a warrant, in the circumstances was unnecessary. Mrs. Pankhurst at first declined to move, but, after a short conversation with the police officers, went on board a special tender that they had chartered to take her ashore. At her urgent request she was accompanied by Mrs. Rheta Child-Dorr, an American journalist and personal friend.

The tender on which the police had embarked unnoticed, at a Devonport quay, proceeded on leaving the Majestic, not to the Great Western Docks, Plymouth, the usual place for ocean passengers to land, but steamed up the Hamoaze about three miles to Bull Point, the Government explosives depot for Plymouth Naval Station. There were in waiting two motor-cars. One was entered by Mrs. Pankhurst and her friend, the Chief Constable, and a Scotland Yard officer, and in the other travelled the Plymouth police matron and four police-constables. Mrs. Pankhurst had not been allowed to bring away with her any of her baggage.

On leaving Bull Point, from which the public are at all times rigidly excluded, the cars proceeded across country by way of Tamerton Folliot until the main road from Plymouth to London was reached. Then the route taken was through Yelverton and across Dartmoor, passing Princetown and Moreton Hampstead, and the cars arrived at Exeter at a quarter past three, Mrs. Pankhurst being lodged in the county gaol.

Anticipating that Mrs. Pankhurst would be landed at the Great Western Docks, a large crowd had assembled there. A Suffragist band played, and Mrs. Flora Drummond and a bodyguard of about twenty Suffragists, with motor-cars waiting, were at the Ocean Quay, Devonport, to receive Mrs. Pankhurst in case she should be landed there. At both places considerable irritation was shown when it was realised that the enthusiasts had been outwitted by the police, but there was no hostile demonstration. Miss Grew, addressing the crowd at the Great Western Docks, said the plan which had been adopted was proof that a miserably weak Government dared not face the Plymouth public and arrest Mrs. Pankhurst ashore.

Emmeline Pankurst's fight led to the Representation of the People Act in 1918 and, for the first time, women were allowed to vote. Pankhurst died in 1928 and was commemorated two years later by a statue that was unveiled in London's Victoria Tower Gardens.

Pearl, Cora

Cora Pearl was said to have been born in Caroline Place, Stonehouse, on 23 February 1842; however, it is believed that she forged her birth certificate and was actually born in London in 1835. Her family moved to Plymouth in 1837. She was born Emma Elizabeth Crouch and would become a famous courtesan of the French demimonde in the nineteenth century.

Pearl had inherited her musical talent from her father, Frederick Nicholas Crouch, a composer and cellist. In 1867, she appeared in the role of Cupid in a production of Jacques Offenbach's *Orpheus in the Underworld*.

A portrait of Cora Pearl. (Courtesy of Seriyrotik1970 under Creative Commons 2.0)

While working in London she became involved in prostitution and had dalliances with several wealthy men. She became the mistress of Robert Bignell, who owned the Argyll Rooms in Regent Street. Together they travelled to Paris where she first adopted the name Cora Pearl. She fell in love with Paris and refused to return to London with Bignell.

Pearl began a theatrical career in Paris but was more known for her sexual appeal than her acting talents. Her theatrical reputation grew and she was soon linked with several wealthy men, including the Duke of Rivoli. While she was with him she developed a serious gambling habit and Rivoli, tired of bailing her out, eventually ended their affair. She soon attracted other rich and powerful men who became her benefactors.

A skilled craftsman could earn between 2 and 4 francs a day, whereas Cora earned 5,000 a night. She was famous for dancing nude on a carpet of orchids and bathing before guests in a silver tub of champagne. The Duke of Grammont-Caderousse said at the time, 'If the Freres Provencaux served an omelette with diamonds in it, Cora would be there every night.'

Her lovers included Prince Willem of Orange, Prince Achille Murat and the Duke of Morny. Morny was Napoleon III's half-brother. Being financially sound, she rented Château de Beauséjour in 1864, which lay on the banks of the Loiret outside Orleans.

When Morny died in 1865 Cora became the mistress of Prince Napoleon, the cousin of Emperor Napoleon III. He purchased two homes in Paris for her and also supported her financially until 1874.

Although her activities made her very wealthy, her downfall resulted from her compulsive gambling and, ultimately, her age. One story though seems to have led more to her downfall than others. She was the mistress of the wealthy Alexandre Duval who lavished her with gifts and money. When she chose to end the affair Duval was so distraught that he shot himself on her doorstep. Rather than call for assistance or help him, she went back inside and went to bed. Duval survived, but stories of the incident spread quickly and brought her theatrical career to a halt. She fled back to London, but her popularity had waned, and she eventually returned to Paris. With no benefactor to support her, she had to sell her possessions to support herself. In 1886, she became ill with intestinal cancer and had to move to a shabby boarding house where she died in poverty and forgotten by most.

Philpott, Putty

Putty Philpott was at one time a very well-known figure in the city. He led the Plymouth, Stonehouse and Devonport Carnival, which raised money for the Royal Albert Hospital (later Devonport Hospital). The carnival lasted all week and Putty was often the carnival king. Regular events included fancy dress competitions, parades and stalls. He was known as a giant of a man, although this referred to his generosity as well as to his weight. He was an ex-navy man and also an ex-publican and, at 20 stone, was once the heaviest man in the services. After leaving the navy, he ran

Putty Philpott cutting the ribbon at the start of the carnival at Pembroke Street, Devonport.

Putty Philpott at the Devonport Carnival.

the Brunswick Hotel in Stonehouse and would entertain people by playing the banjo beside the log fire there. Stars from the Palace Theatre would come to watch and would join in with his many songs, including 'South of the Border down Stonehouse Bridge Way', which he adapted from the better known 'South of the Border'.

During the Second World War, the Brunswick Hotel was destroyed by a land mine. Putty then became the landlord of a pub in Devonport, which, by coincidence, was bombed on his very first night there. He ended his days as the landlord of the No Place Inn at Eldad Hill. In between running various pubs Putty also appeared in concerts performing his many songs, which included 'Figgy Pudding'. It is said that when he died the pall bearers had to be 'fortified at the local bar' before carrying out their bulky task.

Plympton Castle

An ancient settlement built by the Damnonii once stood where Plympton Castle stands today. Their defences were later fortified by the Romans. During the ninth century the Saxons built a small wooden fort at Plympton to defend themselves during raids on the south coast by the Danish. The area was given over to Richard de Redvers, the Earl of Devon, after the Norman Conquest and he built a motte-and-bailey castle on the spot sometime in the early 1100s. His son Baldwin sided with Queen Matilda against King Stephen in 1136 and Stephen sent a large force of men to the castle who seized it and burnt it to the ground. Five years after the event, Baldwin had the castle rebuilt in stone in a circular shape on top of the motte.

In 1204, the castle was confiscated by King John and, through marriage, eventually belonged to Fawkes de Breaute, a soldier and royal servant who had been knighted in 1207. When the king died in 1216 de Breaute swore his loyalties to Henry III and fought at the Battle of Lincoln, where rebel barons, together with Prince Louis of France, had planned to defeat the king.

When de Breaute later argued with Hubert de Burgh, the Earl of Kent and one of the king's key magnates, it resulted in his loss of power, and in 1224 de Burgh ordered him to give up both the castle at Plympton as well as one at Bedford. De Breaute refused and King Henry sent an army to take the castle, which fell after fifteen days. De Breaute fled overseas and into exile.

The castle was still used well into the fourteenth century when it was owned by the Courtenay family. Their estates, including the castle, were acquired by the Crown in 1539. The castle went unused for many years until the outbreak of the Civil War in 1642, eventually being used as the headquarters for the Royalist forces. It continued to be occupied by them until they were forced to withdraw in 1644. The site was abandoned thereafter and its ruins remain on top of a hill beside a small park.

Below left: The remains of Plympton Castle.

Below right: Looking up over the rooftops towards Plympton Castle.

Queen Anne's Battery

In 1667, eastwards of the entrance to Sutton Pool, an open artillery battery was built that was later named after Queen Anne, who reigned from 1702 to 1714. During the Second World War, the US navy had a base at Queen Anne's Battery. A marina lies on the site today.

Queen's Messengers

The Queen's Messengers Convoy were a familiar sight in and around Plymouth during the Second World War. The organisation was set up to feed the homeless and supply warm food and drink to people without electric and water supplies. The Queen's Messenger Food Convoys were named after Queen Elizabeth (the mother of today's Queen Elizabeth), who donated money for the first eighteen convoys.

The Queen's Messengers at Central Park.

R

Robin Hood

Robin Hood wasn't from Plymouth, but the actor who played him in the television series in the 1950s was. Richard Greene was born in Stonehouse on 25 August 1918. He appeared in *The Adventures of Robin Hood* for 143 episodes between 1955 and 1960.

His aunt was Evie Greene, an actress in musical theatre, and his parents were both actors with the Repertory Theatre in Plymouth. He was educated in Kensington and left school when he was eighteen. His stage career began when he played a spear carrier in a version of *Julius Caesar* in 1933. In 1936, he joined the Jevan Brandon Repertory Company and appeared in Terence Rattigan's *French Without Tears* where he came to the attention of Alexander Korda and Darryl F. Zanuck. When he was twenty, he joined 20th Century Fox and became a huge success after appearing in John Ford's *Four Men and a Prayer*. He received so much fan mail that he rivalled Tyrone Power and Robert Taylor. Greene continued to make films until he enlisted in the 27th Lancers during the Second World War.

Greene appeared in propaganda films during the war and also toured entertaining the troops. However, the war ruined Greene's rising film career, although he is well remembered for *Forever Amber*, which was made in 1947. Afterwards, he found himself cast in mainly swashbuckling roles. With little film work and his divorce from Patricia Medina, Greene was almost forgotten when he was approached by Yeoman Films, who offered him the lead role in *The Adventures of Robin Hood*. By taking the role it solved his financial problems and also made him a huge star.

Richard Greene died at his home in Norfolk on 1 June 1985.

Stonehouse-born Richard Greene
as Robin Hood.

Romans

Plymouth didn't exist when the Romans created Exeter, although there is evidence that they once occupied the area. Roman Way, leading downwards from Kings Tamerton, is said to have been the route that the Romans took on their way to Cornwall. A Roman signalling station is thought to have existed at the top of the hill. Roman Way was previously called Old Wall's Lane in the 1800s, which would suggest an earlier settlement. The area was excavated in 1934 by Mr E. N. Masson Phillips, who discovered an early fortification. Soapwort has also been found growing nearby, which was a herb used by the Romans and is usually only found on the site of an old settlement.

Many people believe that Stonehouse got its name from an ancient stone house, now long gone, which once stood in the area. Stonehouse was named by the Saxons, who must have been referring to the ruin of a previous civilisation. If that was the case, then only the Romans would have had the ability to build it. The Romans left Britain in AD 410.

Roman Way lies on the second oldest route traceable in Plymouth, which travels east to west from Saltash to Plympton. There seems to be no record of Roman coins being found at Roman Way, although a hoard of Roman coins was found at Compton Giffard in 1894 and this lies on the same route. The hoard contained a thousand coins – none later than AD 280. It was suggested by the British Museum that the coins could have been used to pay the Romans who were stationed in the area at the time. A similar hoard was found at Marazion, near Penzance. Roman coins have also been found at Whitleigh and by the River Plym. In the early 1980s, the *Evening Herald* reported the find of a Roman coin on the shores of the River Plym. The article read:

> Eighteen hundred years ago this coin must have been lost on the shores of the River Plym. It has been identified as a bronze 'as' and depicts on one side Antoninus Pius, who was Emperor of Rome from 138 to 161 AD, and on the other, Annona, the goddess of the corn-harvest.
>
> This valuable clue to Plymouth's past was found recently, in the mud of the River Plym near Marsh Mills, by Peter Jones, 15, of Efford who was digging not for Romans but for worms.

Royal Naval Hospital

With no long-standing naval hospital in Plymouth Dock and only a hospital ship, the *Canterbury*, the decision was made to build a permanent hospital in the area. In 1756, a piece of land called No Place Field on the southern side of Stonehouse Creek was purchased by the commissioners for sick and wounded seamen. The land was bought from Henry Tolcher, but proved too small and was left undeveloped for sixty-eight years.

In 1758, the commissioners purchased five fields from the Mount Edgcumbe family at a cost of £2,239, 17s and 16d. The fields lay between No Place Field and the creek.

The Millfields, once the Royal Naval Hospital.

Work commenced on the building of the hospital and by 1760, a small part of it was opened for patients. Previously, sick and wounded seamen had been cared for in a building in George Street in Stonehouse.

In 1762, the patients that had been receiving treatment on the *Canterbury* were moved to the new buildings within the hospital. The piece of land at No Place Field that remained unused became the Royal Naval Hospital Burial Ground in 1824.

In 1830, a native from Terra Del Fuego was buried within the grounds of the hospital. He was one of four men brought back to England on HMS *Beagle* by Captain Robert Fitzroy in the same year. The twenty-four-year old native who Fitzroy had named 'Boat Memory' had earlier been transferred to the hospital and he, and the other three natives, later unfortunately all died of smallpox.

Seamen who died from their wounds at the hospital were buried on the grounds, and the last burial took place in 1897. The were no burials within the grounds after that time, apart from one exception: in 1912, the wife of Staff Captain Moore was allowed to be buried with her late husband.

During the Second World War, twenty-four bombs landed on the hospital. One block was totally destroyed and two others were severely damaged.

When the burial ground was acquired by the St Dunstan's Abbey School in 1956, the area was used as a playing field and the headstones were placed around the boundary wall. In later years the hospital continued to treat naval personnel, as well as civilian patients. The hospital was closed in 1995 and today houses Millfields, an upmarket gated community with its own security guards.

Royal William Yard

Work commenced on the Royal William Victualling Yard in 1826. It was designed by Sir John Rennie to be used by the Admiralty as a victualling base for the Royal Navy. The whole site covered an area of 16 acres, including 6 acres of land that were recovered from the sea.

The cost of the yard was approximately £2 million, and it was completed in 1835. By then, the Duke of Clarence had succeeded to the throne and had become William IV. By order of the Admiralty, in 1833 it was named the Royal William Victualling Yard after William IV, the last Lord High Admiral.

A statue of William IV stands over the grand entrance of the yard in Cremyll Street. The statue stands at 13 feet 9 inches and is surrounded by sculptures of the trades that were once incorporated within the yard, including bakers, coopers and butchers.

The many sailing vessels at Royal William Yard.

The grounds of Royal William Yard.

St Andrew's Church

Before the war, St Andrew's Church was located on the southern side of Bedford Street. A church is believed to have stood on this spot since before 1264. The tower dates from 1461 and the labour to build it was paid for by a wealthy local merchant, Thomas Yogge.

St Andrew's was known as the mother church of Plymouth, and William de la Stane was the first recorded vicar there in 1264. It is the largest parish church in Devon and is 184 feet long and 69 feet wide.

The church was badly damaged during the Blitz in 1941 and remained a garden church for many years before being rebuilt in 1957. The morning after St Andrew's Church was bombed in the Second World War, someone placed a wooden sign over the north door with the word 'Resurgam', meaning 'I will rise again'. The word is now carved in stone above the main door.

St Andrew's Church close to Royal Parade.

The interior of St Andrew's Church.

Scott, Robert Falcon

Robert Falcon Scott was born in Plymouth on 6 June 1868. He was a British naval officer and explorer who led two expeditions to Antarctica. The first, the Discovery Expedition, lasted three years and began in 1901. His second expedition, the Terra Nova Expedition, which commenced in 1910, is better known and was the expedition in which he lost his life.

Scott led the team of five men in a race to be the first to reach the South Pole. When he arrived, on 17 January 1912, he discovered that he had been beaten to the position by the Norwegian Roald Amundsen and his team. Scott and his team – which included Edward Wilson, H. R. Bowers, Lawrence Oates and Edgar Evans – made their way back but died of a combination of the cold, hunger and exhaustion.

Scott was born at Outlands House, the family home, in the parish of Stoke Damerel. He was a distant descendant of Sir Walter Scott and he was the father of the naturalist Peter Scott. Outlands has now gone and St Bartholomew's Church on Outlands Road stands in its place. Within the church is a piece of wood bearing Scott's name. In 1908, Scott had carved his name on a tree at Outlands, from where the wood was taken.

Below left: Robert Falcon Scott writing his journal. (Courtesy of the Library of Congress)

Below right: The plaque commemorating Robert Falcon Scott at Outland Road.

Scott was forty-three when he died and his body and that of his comrades remain at the camp where he was found. A wooden cross was erected on top of a high cairn of snow that covered the camp. A memorial stands to Scott at Mount Wise in Devonport.

Smeaton's Tower

Smeaton's Tower is the key landmark on Plymouth Hoe. It was built by John Smeaton on the Eddystone Reef in 1759. There had been two previous lighthouses on the reef. The first was built by Henry Winstanley in 1695. Unfortunately, seven years later during a storm it was washed away, taking its builder with it.

The second lighthouse was built in 1711 by John Rudyerd but was destroyed by a fire in 1755. Work commenced on Smeaton's Tower in December 1756 to replace the damaged lighthouse. Smeaton's Tower would still be there today but the rock underneath it was undermined by the sea. James Douglass built a new lighthouse on an adjoining rock. It was felt that if Smeaton's Tower was left standing beside the new lighthouse it could eventually collapse onto the new one if the rock beneath it became even more undermined. It was decided to blow it up, but Mr F. J. Webb suggested that it should be dismantled and erected on the Hoe where the Trinity House Navigational Obelisk once stood. This was quite a task, but the lighthouse was removed stone by stone and rebuilt on the Hoe with a new base to support it. The original base can still be seen out to sea, beside the present Eddystone Lighthouse.

On 24 September 1884, the Lord Mayor opened Smeaton's Tower on the Hoe to the public.

Below left: The imposing Smeaton's Tower on Plymouth Hoe.

Below right: The lantern house of Smeaton's Tower.

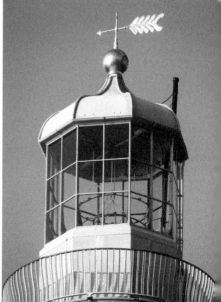

Stoke Gibbet

The tale of the Stoke gibbet is a dark and macabre one. It is a true story that tells of the murder of a dockyard clerk on the night of 21 July 1787. Philip Smith was brutally bludgeoned to death near to Stoke Church. His murderer, John Richards, together with an accomplice, William Smith, were both soon apprehended. Richards was a dock worker who had earlier been suspected of killing a Fore Street sentinel. At first there were no clues as to who had committed the atrocity, but Richards soon boasted of the crime and was arrested shortly afterwards. However, there was little evidence against him and he was soon released. A hat found beside the body was identified as belonging to Richards' accomplice William Smith. Hearing of this, Smith fled to Dartmouth but was soon caught and admitted to his role in the murder and implicated Richards. Both men were tried for murder at Heavitree. They were found guilty, condemned to death and executed in 1788.

The judge in the case, Judge Buller, declared that their bodies wouldn't be given to surgeons for dissection, which was usually the case, but they were to be 'suspended between Heaven and Earth as they were fit for neither'.

The corpses were brought from Exeter to Stoke and displayed near the scene of the crime – a gruesome practice common at the time. The bodies were hoisted in wire cages and chains on a gibbet erected on the muddy Deadlake beach just below Stoke Church. Smith's body stayed there for seven years before the gibbet collapsed, and Richards' body stayed there slightly longer. People avoided the spot, which was said to be 'the terror of some and the disgust of many'. Nettleton's *Stranger's Guide to Plymouth* says that the gibbet stood in place upwards of thirty-eight years near the mill bridge until it was blown down in the gale of 1827.

In 1788 *The Genuine Account of the Trial of Richards and Smith* became a bestseller, selling 25,000 copies. Some were sold around the base of the gibbet.

Stoke Damerel Church close to where the Stoke Gibbet once stood.

Long after the gibbet disappeared, people shunned the area after dark, which, during the 1830s, left the area quiet enough for grave robbers to carry out their grim practices in the secluded Stoke churchyard.

Stonehouse Bridge

Before the Stonehouse Bridge was built, the only way to cross the river was by ferry or by taking the road around Millbridge. Lord Mount Edgcumbe, who was the lord of the manor of Stonehouse, was authorised by an Act of Parliament to construct a bridge linking Devonport and Stonehouse in 1767. He was joined in the venture by Sir John St Aubyn, who was lord of the manor of Stoke Damerel.

The bridge was opened in 1773 and the toll for pedestrians was a halfpenny, which led to the bridge being called Halfpenny Bridge. A cart drawn by one horse was charged a return fare of 2*d*, which increased to 3*d* for two horses and 6*d* for wagons with more than two horses.

The approach to the bridge was via Stonehouse Lane, which later became King Street, and High Lane. Union Street wasn't built until 1815.

The General Tolls Company Ltd bought the rights to the fares taken on the bridge in 1890 for £122,000 – an incredible amount at the time. The Earl of Mount Edgcumbe and Lord St Levan both had shares in the company. An Act of Parliament in 1923 allowed Plymouth Town Council to purchase the toll rights for a sum of £100,000.

The bridge was destroyed by enemy bombing during the Second World War but was later rebuilt. In 1972, the creek was partly filled in with 600,000 tons of rubble, which allowed 19 acres of recreational land to be created.

Stonehouse Bridge today. In 1909, Harry Houdini jumped off the bridge in chains into the cold waters below before quickly making his escape.

Titanic

On 28 April 1912, *Titanic* survivors were brought back to Millbay Docks – fourteen days after the ship had sunk. At 8 a.m. the SS *Lapland* moored at Cawsand Bay with the 167 members of the *Titanic* who hadn't been detained in New York for the American inquiry. Three tenders left Millbay Docks to collect the passengers and the 1,927 sacks of mail that had been scheduled to be carried by the *Titanic*. The third tender, the *Sir Richard Grenville*, carrying the survivors, killed time in the Sound while the dock labourers and porters were paid off and escorted out of the dock gates at West Hoe. After midday the tender was given the all clear and the survivors were allowed to disembark in an air of secrecy. They were then put on a special train from Millbay Docks to Southampton where they arrived at 10.10 p.m. that night.

RMS *Titanic* on its fateful voyage in 1912.

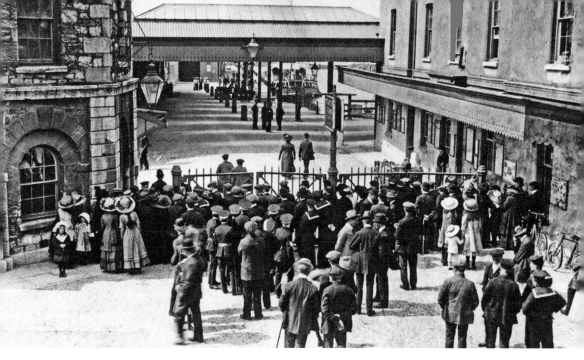

The *Titanic* survivors disembarking at Millbay Docks.

Trams

Transport played a big part in linking the three towns. Plymouth's first tramway was opened in 1872 by the Plymouth, Stonehouse & Devonport Tramways Company. Before the advent of electricity, the trams were pulled by horses. The 4-foot-8-inch-wide track ran from Derry's Clock, along Union Street, over Stonehouse Bridge and ended at Cumberland Gardens in Devonport. In 1874, the line was extended

Below left: The No. 15 tram at Devonport.

Below right: The No. 6 tram heading towards the theatre by Derry's Clock.

to run to Fore Street in Devonport. Electric trams took over from the horse-drawn ones in the early 1900s, and the service eventually covered most of the area known today as Plymouth.

In 1923, the line was extended from St Budeaux along a track that had been closed since the First World War. The trip from the Pier to Saltash Passage covered a remarkable 9 miles and was the longest journey in the city. The fare was 4*d*.

By 1922, motor buses were running in the city and trams became a less viable proposition. In 1941, only the tramline from Drake's Circus to Peverell was still in use, but this was discontinued after the war. The city's last tram ran on 29 September 1945.

Turnchapel

Turnchapel was originally known as St Anne's or Tan Chapel. The area once had two shipyards as well as a private dock, built by Lord Morley of Saltram in 1797. The Plymouth & Dartmoor Railway was in operation here between 1896 and 1951. In 1899, the Oreston & Turnchapel Steamboat Company commenced. Their boats included the *Lively*, *Dart* and *Swift*, which operated from Phoenix Wharf.

Today, much of the older village of Turnchapel still exists, while the waterfront area is occupied by a busy marina.

Above left: The view of the harbour at Turnchapel looking towards Plymouth's city centre.

Above right: The Boringdon Arms at Turnchapel.

U

Union Street

John Foulston designed Union Street in 1811 to link Plymouth with its neighbours – Devonport and Stonehouse. Union Street was constructed in 1815. It had previously been called New Road and the area had formerly consisted of marshland called Sourepool. John Foulston designed the street, incorporating the distinct feature of the Octagon. The street united the three towns of Plymouth, Devonport and Stonehouse. It ran from Derry's Clock to the junction of Manor and Phoenix Street.

Union Street with the Palace Theatre on the left.

It then became Union Street, East Stonehouse, and stretched to the junction at Brownlow Street. It then joined Edgcumbe Street until it met the Stonehouse Bridge. It incorporated Union Terrace, Lockyer Terrace, the Octagon, Squire Terrace, Devonshire Terrace, Flora Place and Sussex Place.

In 1872, Plymouth's first tramway along Union Street was opened. It was controlled by the Plymouth, Stonehouse & Devonport Tramway Company and formed part of a direct link between the three towns.

To make way for the New Palace Theatre of Varieties in the late 1890s, several buildings in Union Street were knocked down. These included premises belonging to Frederick Charles Burner, the tobacconist; Mark Durbin, a provision dealer; Jonathan Crowl, the butcher; and John Shepheard, a bootmaker.

There used to be a turnpike at the Phoenix and Manor Street junction and also a toll booth on the Stonehouse Bridge; however, this ended in 1843 when the Stonehouse Turnpike Trust was dissolved.

For a while Union Street was the home of the wealthy, and a guidebook from 1823 stated:

> The buildings are neat and handsome, and the streets straight and commodious, particularly those of Durnford Street, Emma Place, Edgcumbe Street and Union Street. These are almost entirely occupied by genteel families, chiefly those of naval and military officers, and other persons holding situations under government. The addition of Union Street is an improvement of the greatest importance, it affords a spacious thoroughfare, and presents a succession of neat and uniform buildings.

In 1849, a cholera epidemic broke out in Union Street that was believed to have been caused by works at the nearby Millbay station, which led to blocked drains and caused the overflow of sewerage into nearby homes.

The area has changed greatly over the years, and the street was damaged in the Second World War. Today it looks rather worse for wear, with most of the older buildings removed although several still survive.

V

Victoria Park

Between 1870 and 1899, the area known as 'Deadlake' or 'Stoke Damerel Flete', inhabited by saltmarshes, was slowly converted into what was eventually to become Victoria Park. Bill Parsons, a local man who was a sewerman by trade, dug several pits 18 feet apart. Ladders were placed down manholes to stop men from being swept away while the work was carried out.

The Deadlake had been considered a great health hazard so the land was purchased from the Earl of Mount Edgcumbe in 1890. During 1895, 400 tons of rubble were deposited in the lake and this process continued until 1906.

The park was officially opened in 1903 by the Mayor of Plymouth, Mr J. A. Bellamy. A total of 6,000 people turned up to witness the event and thirty policemen were in attendance. The music was supplied by the Royal Marines band and the festivities concluded with a cricket match.

Virginia House

In 1925, Lord and Lady Astor established the Virginia House Settlement, occupying buildings in Looe Street. Included in the settlement were a meeting room, a gymnasium, a billiard and social room along with a library, music room and a dance hall. In smaller rooms there were lessons for cookery, carpentry and dressmaking as well as singing classes. Writing classes were held in the library. The settlement also promoted many clubs and societies. These included a mothers' club, a youth club, a men's club, a football team and a boxing club. Lord Astor also set up the World Order Group where members could discuss international affairs.

Between 1941 and 1952, members could take holidays at Princetown after the Astors leased a building there for the purpose.

The settlement still survives but a number of buildings have been sold off, with the organisation investing the money to fund grants to local charities.

The entrance to Virginia House in Peacock Lane.

W

Wild West

When Buffalo Bill visited Plymouth on 3 June 1904, he brought with him a troop of Native Americans who toured with his Wild West Show. For the first time American Indians could be seen sitting on street corners in the Stonehouse and Union Street areas of the city. This proved to be an amazing sight to people whose only experience of the Wild West was through the various stories that appeared in daily newspapers and comics. Children were particularly fascinated by the American Indians, their only knowledge of them being from tales told about Geronimo or Custer's last stand.

The one thing that was noted at the time about the visiting American Indians was that they couldn't handle their drink, and notices appeared in drinking houses that read, 'No Indians to be served.' Nowadays this might seem to appear racist, but at the time the problem was actually caused by the Native Americans becoming drunk too quickly and being overly rowdy.

Sitting Bull and Buffalo Bill in 1885. (Courtesy of the Library of Congress)

Willie Sitting Bull was one of the American Indians who accompanied Buffalo Bill to Britain. He was the only son of Sitting Bull. Sitting Bull himself had originally taken part in the show when it had toured America. Willie regularly took part in mock battles, which featured the defeat of Custer at Little Big Horn. The show took place at the Exhibition Fields, Pennycomequick, just at the bottom of what is today Central Park.

Winstanley, Henry

Henry Winstanley was born in 1644 and was an English painter and engineer who was responsible for constructing the first Eddystone Lighthouse after two of his ships were lost on the Eddystone Rocks.

He was a merchant and invested some of the money he'd made in five ships. When two of his vessels were destroyed on the Eddystone Rocks, near Plymouth, he questioned why nothing had been done to protect ships sailing near to the hazard. When he was informed that the reef was too dangerous to mark he decided to construct a lighthouse there himself; he was supported by the Admiralty, who supplied ships and men.

Work began on 14 July 1696 to a design that included an octagonal tower built from Cornish granite and wood as well as a glass lantern room where candles supplied the light needed to safely guide in passing vessels. The anchor for the lighthouse was provided by twelve iron stanchions fixed securely to the rock. Because Britain and France were at war at the time, a naval vessel was assigned to protect the men who were working on the reef. In June 1697, the commissioner at Plymouth, George St Lo, ordered the protection vessel to join the fleet but failed to provide a replacement. This allowed a French privateer to destroy the work completed so far on the foundations. The privateer captured Winstanley, taking him back to France; however, Louis XIV ordered his immediate release, stating, 'France is at war with England, not with humanity.' Winstanley made his way back to the reef and work on the lighthouse continued. It was completed in November 1698.

A portrait of lighthouse builder Henry Winstanley.

In the winter of 1698–99 the lighthouse suffered damage due to bad weather. The light was often obscured by sea spray, which led to Winstanley rebuilding it on a larger scale the following spring. It included more stonework together with elaborate decoration. The lighthouses were a success and there were no shipwrecks for the five years in which they were in operation.

Winstanley had great faith in his lighthouse, stating that he would like to be in it during 'the greatest storm there ever was'. On the night of 27 November 1703, he got his wish. Winstanley was visiting the structure to make repairs when the lighthouse was destroyed in the Great Storm, taking the tower and its builder out to sea.

Wyndham Square

Wyndham Square was developed in the 1830s as part of John Foulston's major development of the area between Plymouth and Stonehouse.

Originally the square surrounded a Nonconformist chapel, which was replaced by St Peter's Church (built between 1880 and 1882). Terraces were built to the north and south of the square. Densham Terrace was completed by 1848 followed by the development to the east side of Cecil Street.

Arundel Crescent was developed by 1865 and much of the area between Arundel Crescent, Wyndham Street East and Archer Terrace was completed by 1867. The area around Wolsdon Street and Wyndham Street West was developed by 1881.

Founded in 1900, St Boniface's was run by the Presentation Brothers from Ireland. The building is still there, on the approach towards the front of the church.

Extensively damaged in the Second World War during the Blitz in 1941, St Peter's Church in Wyndham Square was rebuilt by Frederick Etchells in 1955 and reconsecrated in 1956. Between 2004 and 2007 the church was renovated. Many of the nearby properties are Grade II listed and during the last century some were reported to be haunted.

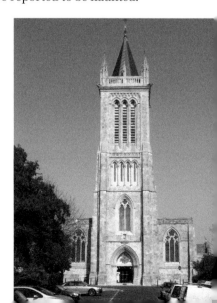

St Peter's Church at Wyndham Square.

Xmas Ship

In November 1914, America sent a ship full of Christmas gifts for war orphans in Plymouth. American newspapers reported on 26 November that the 'Santa Claus Ship' was met with much joy and that Plymouth and Devonport had been festooned with decorations to welcome the Americans. Huge crowds gathered to meet the *Jason* as warships directed it into the harbour. Lord Kitchener sent a message expressing the army's gratitude, which was read at a banquet to the ship's officers.

The ship was loaded with 8,000 tons of gifts comprising of 5 million separate articles that had been donated by American children and were destined for British, Belgian, French, German and Austrian children whose fathers were away fighting in the war.

The ship was officially welcomed by Earl Beauchamp, the president of the council, on behalf of the government. He was accompanied by Mr F. D. Acland, the Under-Secretary of Foreign Affairs, together with a large gathering of naval and military officers.

The USS *Jason*, the Christmas Ship, during the First World War.

Among the greetings awaiting the ship was one from the queen to the wife of the American ambassador. In her letter, the queen wrote:

> I am anxious to express through you my warm appreciation of this touching proof of generosity and sympathy and to ask you to be so kind as to convey my heartfelt thanks to all who have contributed towards these presents, which will, I am sure, be gladly welcomed by the children for whom they are intended and received with gratitude by their parents.

The scheme was initiated by the *Chicago Herald* and a Mr O'Loughlin, who represented the journal, stated that 200 other newspapers throughout the United States had assisted in the project. As well as an enormous collection of toys, gifts also included shoes, boots, clothing, sweaters and stockings. So much was collected that 100,000 tons of presents had to be left behind.

While the *Jason* was at Plymouth, gifts were left for British and Belgian children before the ship carried on its journey to Marseilles to deliver presents to German children. It then carried on to Genoa to distribute gifts to further German and Austrian children. Gifts heading for Russia were loaded on to a different vessel.

YMCA

In 1844, George Williams founded the YMCA and held its first meeting in Plymouth in 1848. Williams visited Plymouth again in 1887 to open a new YMCA at No. 14 Bedford Street and established a YMCA at Devonport three years later. During the First World War, the association opened a servicemen's hostel in Union Street

The YMCA providing tea for the troops in Plymouth during the Second World War.

as well as extending its work across the Channel to help serving troops by supplying food and drink from special YMCA marquees, as well as providing writing paper and envelopes.

During the Second World War, the organisation opened a canteen in Devonport for servicemen in 1940. The following year, during the Blitz in Plymouth in 1941, the YMCA headquarters at Old Town Street was destroyed. Its hostel at Lockyer Street received a direct hit, which resulted in the deaths of five staff, three residents and three visitors. Afterwards, the YMCA relocated to Peverell Park Villa.

The YMCA continued to grow after the war with, eventually, branches all over the world. Today, YMCA Plymouth is located at Honicknowle Lane.

Yogge, Thomas

Thomas Yogge was a wealthy merchant who was responsible for the building of the Prysten House in 1498. The tower of St Andrew's Church, which stands at 136 feet, was also funded by Thomas Yogge, as was the Lady Chapel on the north of the church.

In 1501, Yogge, who was involved in the French wine trade, gave a hogshead of claret that was presented to Catherine of Aragon when she arrived in Plymouth from Spain after a difficult voyage across the Channel. Catherine travelled to England to marry Arthur, Prince of Wales. At Plymouth, she travelled to St Andrew's to give thanks for her safe journey.

The Prysten House was built using Plymouth limestone and Dartmoor granite. Today the building is owned by Plymouth City Council and in the past has been used as a museum as well as a restaurant.

Thomas Yogge died in 1509.

The Prysten House built by Thomas Yogge.

Zoo

Plymouth Zoo opened on Thursday 19 April 1962 and cost £30,000 to build. It had 13,000 visitors during its first three days. The zoo was owned by the Chipperfield family and proved to be a very popular attraction for many years.

Animals found at the zoo included chimpanzees, elephants, polar bears, seals, giraffes and bears as well as tortoises, rabbits and guinea pigs in the petting area of

Below left: The much-loved Percy the pelican who happily followed visitors hoping for some extra food.

Below right: Nellie the elephant, a favourite at the zoo.

the zoo. The enclosures were small, concrete and bars, and many felt sorry for the animals. One particular favourite was Percy the pelican, who happily followed visitors around the grounds. During the 1970s, admission was 1s (5p) and there was a large café selling food and drinks as well as souvenirs such as chimpanzee masks, badges and pencils. Oddly, toffee-flavoured popcorn could be bought to feed to the animals.

The zoo closed sixteen years later on Sunday 8 January 1978 and was later converted into a skateboard park before closing altogether soon after.

Right: The giraffe enclosure with Central Park in the background.

Below: Feeding the monkeys at Plymouth Zoo.

Bibliography

Books

Cluer, Andrew, *Plymouth and Plymothians* (Lantern Books, 1975)
Robinson, Chris, *Plymouth in the 70s* (Pen and Ink, 2015)
Robinson, Chris, *Plymouth As Time Draws On* (Pen and Ink, 1985)
Robinson, Chris *Victorian Plymouth* (Pen and Ink, 2016)
Tait, Derek, *Images of Plymouth: Stonehouse* (Driftwood Coast, 2011)
Tait, Derek, *Plymouth Hoe* (Driftwood Coast, 2008)
Tait, Derek, *Plymouth: Tales from the Past* (Driftwood Coast, 2010)

Websites

BBC History, www.bbc.co.uk/devon
Brian Moseley's Old Plymouth, www.oldplymouth.uk
Devonport online, www.devonportonline.co.uk
Plymouth Museums Galleries Archives, plymhearts.org/elizabethan-house

Acknowledgements

Most of the older photos in the book come from the author's collection while the newer photos were either taken by the author or Tina Cole, except for the photo of Plymouth Argyle's ground, which was taken by Andrew Dolan. Thanks to Tina Cole for helping to research this book and thanks also to Tilly Barker.

About the Author

Derek Tait is a full-time author based in Plymouth who has written books on a range of subjects for Amberley Publishing, The History Press and Pen and Sword. Books include *A 1970s Childhood; The Great Houdini: His British Tours; Sampans, Banyans and Rambutans;* as well as a large selection of local history titles.

His website is at www.derektait.co.uk